The Challenges We Face

THE
CHALLENGES
WE
FACE

Edited and compiled from the Speeches and
Papers of **Richard M. Nixon**

McGRAW–HILL BOOK COMPANY, INC.
NEW YORK
TORONTO
LONDON

THE CHALLENGES WE FACE

In 1952 our Republican convention turned to a highly talented man for the Vice-Presidential nomination. None of us has ever regretted that choice. Dick Nixon has been a credit to the Administration, our party, and our country. Since 1952 he has gained nearly eight years of added governmental experience at the highest level—a tour of seasoning unmatched in the nation's history. All of us know him as a man of integrity and deep faith—one who is intelligent, mature, and uniquely knowledgeable in the problems and personalities in the world scene. And along with this, he has that priceless gift, a sense of humor—indispensable in politics.   —Washington, April 4, 1960

There is no man in the history of America who has had such a careful preparation as has Vice President Nixon for carrying out the duties of the Presidency. There hasn't been a principal administrative meeting among the heads of government that he has not attended as an active participant. He has gone on behalf of the United States to many foreign countries. And in every country that he has visited the United States has gained many additional friends. I have called upon him to serve on numerous committees, and the success attained is a tribute to his dedication and to his wisdom.

—Gettysburg, September 12, 1956

Dwight D. Eisenhower

Publisher's Foreword

The Challenges We Face has been compiled and edited from the speeches and papers of Vice President Richard M. Nixon by members of the editorial staff of the McGraw-Hill Book Company with the aid and assistance of Mr. Nixon's staff and with the Vice President's full authorization.

The material has been arranged and edited topically into twenty-two sections grouped under five major headings. At the bottom of the first page of each section, the reader will find a complete list of sources for all the material that appears in that section. Nothing in the book predates 1956.

The editing was of a purely mechanical nature. To fit the material into this topical pattern, it was necessary to edit for continuity, to eliminate repetition, and to join materials taken from different sources. Some entire sections—for instance, all four in Part Five having to do with Mr. Nixon's Russian trip—are reprinted here in their original form and absolutely without change. However, other sections that rely in part on press conferences and question-and-answer sessions for material have undergone changes in form but not in content. Also, editing was made inevitable by the transferral of the spoken word to the printed page. The basic materials—ideas, opinions, emphases, and virtually all the words—are Mr. Nixon's, reproduced in the contexts he intended.

Mr. Nixon is donating all of his royalties from *The Challenges We Face* to charity.

THE PUBLISHERS

Contents

PART FIVE

Mission to the Soviet Union

PART ONE

America: Its Heritage and Mission

1. *The Pioneer Spirit* [1]

The American challenge in the next half-century is to fulfill the mission implicit in the great principles that constitute the American revolutionary tradition.

The history books will tell you the American Revolution ended at Yorktown. I do not think this is correct. The American Revolution has not ended, and it will not end, until throughout the world nations have the right to be independent, individuals to be free, and all people to live in peace with their neighbors.

This has always been the American mission. It caught the imagination of the world 165 to 170 years ago. And if we can, during this critical period in world history, rededicate ourselves to those great principles, there is no question but that the American Revolution, which is much bigger than the United States itself, will continue to inspire peoples throughout the world. The American Revolution as we know it is really the way of the future—not the Communist Revolution with its emphasis on dictatorship and atheism and materialism.

These principles go all the way back to the earliest settlements on this continent.

The landing of the *Mayflower* at Plymouth on December 21, 1620, and the settling of the Jamestown colony in 1607 were much more than merely historical events. They have become symbols that express the courage and greatness of those who

---

[1] The material in this section is derived from the following sources:
Remarks at the Oregon Centennial Celebrations, Astoria, Salem, and Portland, Oregon. February 14, 1959. Remarks before the Fourth Annual Luncheon of the General Conference of CBS Television Network Affiliates, Washington, D.C. January 13, 1958. Remarks on Jamestown Day at Jamestown Festival Park, Virginia. May 13, 1957. Remarks at the *Mayflower II* Celebration, Plymouth, Massachusetts. June 22, 1957.

founded on this continent a nation dedicated to the cause of freedom.

I suppose that many of us, at one time or other, have reflected upon the feelings of these early settlers. They left the land of their fathers to undertake a long and dangerous voyage. They came to a land that offered opportunity, but also a land of unknown risk, of fear, of uncertainty. It took both faith and courage to a heroic degree to embark upon this adventure. From these great qualities, combined with the equal heroism of subsequent settlers and immigrants, the spirit of America was born.

Some historians call the first settlement in Jamestown, Virginia, the beginning of the United States of America. One has called it the beginning of the modern world—and certainly we must agree that the settlement which got its foothold at Jamestown opened up a new era in man's mastery of the physical universe.

I believe the events which took place in Jamestown 350 years ago should mean a great deal to us today. For Jamestown was the beginning of a new type of society which was ultimately to revolutionize the life of the average man in both the Old World and the New, and to point a promise of universal enlightenment and well-being undreamed of by Captain John Smith and his brave band.

When I saw replicas of the three ships that carried the first colonists to Jamestown, I realized as never before how greatly the sense of man's individual worth has increased in the 350 years since the new American society began. The dark holds of these three ships, unlighted and unventilated, tell all too clearly how little life held for the average man in 1607. The fact that so many men were willing to brave the hazards of the Atlantic on ships so perilously small reveals how desperately they longed for the opportunity and the dignity that America was to give them and their children.

It was to be a dignity spelled out in terms of the individual.

This is what succeeding generations of Virginians—Nathaniel Bacon, Patrick Henry, Washington, Jefferson, Madison, Mason, Marshall, and countless others—saw with increasing clarity and helped to lead their countrymen toward. This is what Lincoln meant when he called the young republic "the last, best hope of earth" and pinned his confidence for the future to an America with growing opportunity for all.

Beneath the very earth on which Jamestown stands today are buried countless numbers of those who came, lured by these dreams. Tragic and terrible as war is, I venture to say that no battle in which our nation has fought has taken so heavy a toll of the participants as the Jamestown beachhead in the years 1607 to 1610.

And yet, despite loss at sea, famine, disease, and terrible loneliness, they continued to come, both young men and old, laborers and poets, noblemen and ne'er-do-wells, all lured by the vague consciousness that in the uncharted miles of this great, sprawling continent lay not only the certainty of wealth but also the hopes of a new society which promised to them and their descendants a life richer in both spiritual and material values than they had ever known before.

As the Reverend John Donne, dean of St. Paul's in London and chaplain to the London company which settled Jamestown, said in his annual sermon to that company in 1622, "You have made this Island, which is but the suburb of the Old World, a bridge and gallery to the New; to join all to that world that should never grow old, the Kingdom of Heaven."

The courage of the first settlers was duplicated in the courage of the armies of the Revolution. Against incredible obstacles, under the unflagging leadership of George Washington, we won our freedom and independence. A new republic was born. A great experiment in democracy began its electrifying course.

The courage of the settlers and the fighters for independence persisted in their children and in the new immigrants who came to our shores. Slowly our nation pushed on its westward march, across rugged mountains and fertile valleys and plains, across the Mississippi and up the Missouri, through deserts and mountain divides, to the waters of the Pacific. The wagon train moving across the Oregon Trail, Robert Gray sailing into the mouth of the Columbia, Lewis and Clark at Celilo Falls—these great events are legendary and dramatic parts of the tradition and history of our pioneer days which every American cherishes in his heart. We need such vivid reminders of the rugged pioneer spirit of our people, of the tremendous progress we have enjoyed, and of the sense of destiny of this nation.

Let us examine some of the qualities of those who braved the rigors of the tortuous, four-month journey along the Oregon Trail from Independence to Astoria a hundred years ago. There have been many histories written on those who were pioneers in the West. Some are highly romantic accounts, some are cynical treatments that would have us believe all pioneers were neurotics and adventurers.

Others explain this vast migration by the too-simple generalization that most of the pioneers were motivated by rebellion against arbitrary authority and were largely malcontents.

There may be an element of truth in this analysis. But the men who made the West were not an earlier generation of "Angry Young Men" railing out at the world, believing in nothing. They were not taken up with the "Cult of Togetherness," nor were they imbued with the idea of "group adjustment" in a safe and undemanding security. They had the same great qualities which the Pilgrims and the Jamestown settlers had before them and which the American people need in abundance today.

There was, first, an almost incredible capacity for sacrifice and hard work. Why should we be reminded of this today? In the great competition which is taking place between the slave world and the free world we often hear it said that free men can always outproduce slaves. I believe this is true. But we must never forget that it is only true when both work. It is not true when slaves work and free men loaf.

Every visitor to the Soviet Union comments on the immense capacity of the Russian people for hard work and sacrifice to accomplish their national goals. Our economic system is more efficient than theirs, and is in every way superior, but we shall stay ahead only if our people produce to the maximum of their capabilities.

We Americans assert, and rightly so, that our living standards are the highest in the world. They are high in comparison with those of the most advanced industrial nations anywhere. They are high in comparison with our own levels of ten, twenty, or thirty years ago.

This prosperity can mean much in the way of human welfare. It can mean opportunities for better education, the highest quality of medical care, the bringing of cultural gains even to the remotest parts of our land, and finally the leisure to enjoy not only material benefits but also the blessings of family life and companionship.

But our prosperity also brings with it a moral challenge that we cannot overlook. It is the challenge to sustain in prosperity the high qualities of character that we developed in adversity. We know from history that great nations have become corrupt, soft, and decadent under the influence of prosperity. We know that the ancient empire of Rome fell, not primarily because of barbarian attacks, but rather because of the apathy and indifference of a prosperous citizenry. Rome fell when its own people lost the will to fight for their native land.

I raise this point because there are some in our nation today who say that we cannot afford the sacrifices needed to maintain our national security. They oppose foreign aid programs, or even some of our direct costs of defense, because the budget is too high. They say that we cannot continue to carry the burden imposed by the common effort of free nations to keep alive in the world the spirit of freedom and the recognition of the dignity of man.

Certainly I agree that we should vigorously oppose any waste or any unnecessary expenditure of government funds. I respect the integrity of any man who may disagree with any specific program and hold that it does not really contribute to world peace. It is our democratic right and duty to debate the details of our foreign policy and programs.

But I cannot understand the attitude of those who refuse to examine the arguments—who simply say we cannot afford it. No price is too great to pay for freedom. If we were a poor nation, instead of the most prosperous in the history of the world, I would still say that we could afford every dollar that is truly necessary to protect our liberty and to help bring peace to the world.

We are making sacrifices today. Our tax burden is far heavier than any of us would like it to be. But how do our sacrifices compare with those of the Pilgrim Fathers? Are we giving as much as the cold and hungry soldiers at Valley Forge gave? Is the sacrifice of a portion of our income comparable to the sacrifice asked of our soldiers in World War II or in Korea?

A second characteristic of the pioneers was their insatiable spirit of adventure. We Americans could use more of that spirit today.

As we move into the space age there has been too much talk of justifying the effort we are making in this field on the grounds of its potential military usefulness and not enough emphasis on the far more important ground that, if a nation is to achieve and retain greatness, its people must never tire in their efforts to explore the unknown and to acquire knowledge.

The comment we sometimes hear—"why should anybody

want to go to the moon?"—is a sad commentary on the mental attitude of a people who share the splendid heritage of the early settlers and pioneers. If that attitude had prevailed 350 years ago, New England would never have been settled; 100 years ago, and the West would never have been opened. We could also add that if Columbus and his contemporaries had felt that way, America would not have been discovered in the first place!

Another characteristic of the pioneers was that they had unswerving faith, faith in freedom, faith in American ideals, faith in God. We need more of that faith today. We need a spiritual rebirth, a rededication to positive ideals.

For us, as Americans, to rest our case before the world on materialism and missiles alone is in no way worthy of our magnificent heritage. That is why we should talk more of our faith in freedom and less of our fear of communism; more of the promise of the American Revolution and less of the threat of the Communist Revolution. Our message to the world must be that the choice of newly developing countries is not between communism and things as they are, but between things as they are and something infinitely better than communism. The Communists offer progress without freedom. The American idea offers even greater progress—but always with freedom.

In the course of our history we have met grave challenges in war and have never failed to fight through to victory. We have met difficult economic problems and have surmounted them until today we lead the world in income and wealth. We have faced social problems and have made such progress that we can look forward to the day when poverty and destitution will be abolished in our land. We are moving ahead strongly and resolutely to assure racial justice. We do not want in our midst the shame of discrimination and oppression.

The qualities that made possible all of these gains are moral. They reflect character and principle. They can only be explained in terms of the religious traditions that impel us to adopt as our national motto In God We Trust.

I do not see how any believer in God and in the dignity of man can falter in the struggle that faces us. Communism is totally opposed to all that we believe and cherish. We believe in justice and the moral law; they believe in force alone. We preach love and forgiveness; theirs is a message of hatred. To the religious person, every man is sacred, because all were created by a loving God. To the Communist, his fellow man is but a tool to be used in the effort to seek total power. We seek peace; they prepare to conquer. It is these qualities of the spirit that give us confidence for the future.

A final characteristic of our pioneers was that they had a sense of destiny and mission about America. They believed with Lincoln that our Declaration of Independence meant "liberty not alone to the people of this country but hope to the world for all future time." They knew, as he did, that "our defense is in the preservation of the spirit which prizes liberty as the heritage of all men in all lands everywhere."

The revolutionary concept that all men are created equal not only inspired the early American settlers but it inspired the rest of the world. Our task today is to make that same faith inspire the world in the same way once again. This is America's true destiny. In the words of a great Virginian, Woodrow Wilson, "A patriotic American is never so proud of the great flag under which he lives as when it comes to mean to other people as well as to himself the symbol of hope and liberty."

Throughout history men with positive goals, and persistence and faith in those goals, are the ones whose ideas have prevailed. The fearful have always been eventually subdued.

We are challenged in the world today by a tough, skillful, relentless adversary who has total conviction in his faith that communism represents the wave of the future and will eventually dominate the world.

For the Communist no sacrifice is too great, no goal is impossible to attain, no effort too strenuous.

A stand-pat, status-quo, smug, and complacent America cannot prevail against such men as these, regardless of the inherent rightness of its cause.

America today needs the spirit of the Jamestown settlers and the pioneers of the Oregon Trail—the same initiative, the same willingness to work, and above all, the same burning faith in the ideals of the American Revolution.

2. *Our Legacy from the Old World* [2]

No two peoples in the world are more closely bound by a common heritage than the British and the American people. It can in truth be said that we are brothers, united by the strongest ties of history, language, and culture. But it can happen among nations as among families, that brothers can drift apart unless continued and sustained efforts are made to keep alive the sense of heritage which binds them together.

On several occasions since I have held my present office, official visitors from England, including most recently your distinguished Prime Minister, Mr. Macmillan, have spoken graciously of the appreciation of the people of Britain for the assistance received from the United States in the difficult reconstruction days after World War II.

I consider it a privilege to state that what aid we were able to provide was at best a modest payment on a debt which can

[2] The material in this section is derived from the following sources:
Address before the Pilgrims, London, England. November 25, 1958. Address before the English-speaking Union of the Commonwealth, London, England. November 26, 1958. The Toast of the Vice President to Queen Elizabeth II, Washington, D.C. October 18, 1957. Address at the Alfred E. Smith Memorial Dinner, New York, N.Y. October 18, 1956.

never adequately be repaid. For no people in history owe more of their heritage to another than the American people to the British.

There is, first, the English language. While we admittedly speak it a bit imperfectly—so badly in fact that Mr. Shaw's Professor Higgins contends that in America, English has not been spoken for years—we proudly share with you the language of William Shakespeare, of the authors of the King James translation of the Bible, of Pope and Dryden and of countless others whose words are gems of great poetry and noble prose.

There is also the common law—one of the most potent civilizing forces in history. We inherited from you the noble concept that no man was so great that he could be above the law or so mean that he was beneath its protection.

Third, there is the Parliament. Your Parliament has been called, and rightly so, the Mother of Parliaments. In our nation's capital, in our states, and in countless cities, towns and villages, the procedures of our legislative bodies stem directly from our English tradition.

Every time our Congress meets, every time an American judge sits in the majesty of the law, every time our citizens gather to debate their problems—in short, every time an American citizen acts politically within the democratic context—we reflect our English heritage.

It has been my privilege over the past five years to visit with Mrs. Nixon English-speaking nations in all parts of the world— New Zealand and Australia, the colonies of Hong Kong and Singapore, Malaya, Pakistan, India, Ceylon, Ghana, and Canada. We found wide differences in these countries in race, religion, food, clothing, and custom. But we also found that these people, so different in these respects from each other and from Americans, were bound together by these same three great institutions—the Parliament, the common law, and the English language.

And there are more material elements of our debt.

There are the billions of dollars in capital which poured into the United States from Britain during the period when we were an underdeveloped, capital-deficit nation.

During the nineteenth century when we enjoyed the growth that made us a world power, the might and majesty of the Royal Navy kept the freedom of the seas, and the beneficent effects of the Pax Britannica fostered the growth of industry and commerce not only for us but for peoples throughout the world.

Too numerous to mention are the British contributions in the field of inventions. From Watt's steam engine to your jet Comet, from Jenner's smallpox vaccine to Fleming's penicillin, and today the magnificent and exciting work of British scientists in developing the peaceful uses of atomic energy—in these and countless other fields we owe a debt of gratitude to British ingenuity and genius.

And there are other aspects of our debt.

There is our good fortune in having for our northern neighbor a nation with a similar heritage which has enabled us to share the benefits of the longest unguarded international boundary in the world. There are the hundreds of thousands of lives of brave British men who held the line against forces which threatened our independence as well as yours until we were able to join the battle in two world wars.

And there is, finally, the assurance we feel in these difficult times in the fact that the United States has no better or more loyal friends in the world than the United Kingdom and our other allies among the countries that make up the Commonwealth of Nations.

In this regard I should like to mention that much maligned institution, British colonialism. It is understandable in view of the surging rise of nationalism that we have heard all that is bad and little that is good about colonialism in the past few years.

Colonialism has had its faults, but it also has had its virtues. I speak from some knowledge on this subject. I have visited twelve countries which at one time or another have passed through the status of British colonialism. I have known personally and admired the dedicated and effective work of your superb colonial administrators. You can indeed be proud of the contributions that have been made by men like Grantham in Hong Kong, Templer in Kuala Lumpur, MacDonald in Singapore, Crawford in Uganda, and Arden-Clark in Ghana.

Let us examine some of the benefits British colonial policy has produced in the areas in which it has operated. It brought the military strength which provided security from external attack. It brought in many areas the technical training which assured economic progress.

But more important than either of these, it brought the great ideas which provided the basis for future progress—ideas which will live on for generations after the nations concerned have acquired the independent status for which an enlightened policy has prepared them.

The common law, the Parliament, the English language, freedom of speech, assembly, press and religion—these are the institutions which are the proud legacy of the British people in lands throughout the world.

It is appropriate for me as an American during our traditional Thanksgiving season to express appreciation on English soil for the fact that we derived our political system, many of our institutions, and much of our material well-being from a country which has so painstakingly nurtured and safeguarded the fundamental rights of man.

The traditions and customs which we share in common are important in developing the closer understanding we all desire between our peoples. But equally important is awareness of those diversities in our background which might explain different attitudes to our current problems.

No one, for example, would question the fact that both the British and the American people are deeply devoted to the cause of peace. On the other hand, we can well understand why a citizen of London, who gained his experience as to the horror of air attacks by living through them in World War II, might be more concerned over the urgency of reaching agreement on disarmament than a citizen of New York who had experienced those attacks only by reading about them in a newspaper.

There are other reasons as well that explain why we Americans act as we do. I think a thumbnail outline of the elements which make up the American character might serve to explain some of our attitudes.

There is, first, the diversity of our population. Our English traditions come not only from the Pilgrims whom we honor today but also, to mention only some of the others, from the Cavaliers in Virginia, the Catholics in Maryland, and the Quakers in Pennsylvania. And the waves of nineteenth-century immigration brought in Germans, Irish, Italians, Scandinavians, Poles—all the peoples of Europe and of Asia and Africa as well. The mainstream of our tradition is British, but also represented in America are all races, all nations, all religions of the world.

Who are the people of America? Ours is no master race. Our fathers came from all nations and all continents. We are English, Irish, German, Italian, Polish, French. We are European, Asian, African. But first, last, and always—we are Americans.

The result has been a fusion of the best ideals and the strongest energies of all the peoples that have come to our shores. In the "melting-pot" of America we have welcomed all and have shared in the diversity and richness that each has to contribute.

We are strong in our unity, but we are stronger still because of our diversity.

In addition to the diversity of our population there is the diversity which arises from our geography. It is natural that those in the East would be more concerned with the problems of Europe, those in the West with Asia, those in the Southwest with Latin America, and those in the Midwest with national more than international problems.

We are, in truth, a land of many voices. We differ vigorously on many issues. As a result, the voice of the minority may often be mistaken for the voice of America. You may well recall that while the critics of the Marshall Plan made most of the news, those of us who supported it had, fortunately, by far most of the votes.

We are idealistic, perhaps too much so at times, in our approach to international problems.

We did not seek the position of world power in which we find ourselves, and sometimes we may seem to be reluctant in assuming the responsibilities which go with power.

Our relative inexperience in the age-old intricacies of international diplomacy may account for these typical attitudes: We expect quick success for every venture in the foreign policy area. We are intolerant of failures in diplomacy, regardless of the reasons therefor. We are impatient with the inevitable slowness of diplomatic negotiations. We tend to be distrustful of any settlement which smacks of compromise.

Having pointed out our diversity and having admitted some of our weaknesses, it is only accurate to put them in perspective by also recognizing some of our strengths.

With all of our differences, whenever we are confronted with a threat to our security we are not then Republicans or Democrats but Americans; we are not then fifty states but the United States.

Mr. Khrushchev could make no greater miscalculation than to base his policies on his professed conclusion that the 1958 election reflected a lack of confidence in the foreign policy leadership of the President and might therefore bring about a weakening of our determination to resist the aggressive tactics of world communism.

The overwhelming majority of the American people and the responsible leaders of both of our parties continue to support the President in the foreign policy area.

The American government and people want peace. We welcome the opportunity to discuss and settle at the conference table any differences we have with other nations. But we believe that we in the free world could render no greater disservice to the cause of peace than to fail to stand firm—as we have in the Formosa Straits, for example—against the use of aggressive force as a means of settling differences between nations.

I realize that there are many well-intentioned critics of this firm policy both in the United States and in the United Kingdom. Our disagreement is not on ends but on means. We all want peace. The question is how we can best preserve it.

It is our conviction that, in dealing with an international aggressor, rewarding aggression might appear to be the easy way to peace, but it would far more likely prove to be the inevitable way to war. The lesson of history is clear. Rewarding aggression does not stop it; it only encourages more aggression in the future.

I think it is appropriate also to reiterate the position of our government with regard to the various Soviet probing actions directed against Berlin.

When the resolution of the free world is thus tested, we believe it is essential to show our unmistakable determination to stand firm. We have made clear our determination to remain in the city until a German settlement, acceptable to the German people, has been achieved. This is a matter about which there exists no shadow of ambiguity, and I am confident that our two governments will continue to remain united in this policy.

Finally, may I note another of our national characteristics

about which there can be no question? As the unprecedented outpouring of affection of millions of Americans for Her Gracious Majesty Queen Elizabeth II and Prince Philip on the occasion of their visit to the United States so eloquently illustrated, the overwhelming majority of our people in both of our parties are united in their determination to work with our friends and allies in the Commonwealth of Nations toward the common objective of peace and freedom for people throughout the world.

Above all, we must recognize that there is nothing more essential to the preservation of the strength the free world needs in these critical times than the maintenance of the alliance and friendship of the English-speaking peoples. Because we have so much in common, a superficial observer might conclude that there could be no reason for differences to arise between us.

On the contrary, as free and independent nations we recognize that we will not always find ourselves in agreement. We have had our differences in the past, but they have only served to increase our determination to work more closely together in the future. And I am happy to be able to observe that due to the diligent efforts of Prime Minister Macmillan and President Eisenhower, and others on both sides of the ocean, the United Kingdom and the United States stand today more closely united in purposes and policies than at any time since World War II.

What is the unfinished work left for our generation? I believe that two American Presidents speaking in this same Guildhall have simply, but eloquently, answered that question.

Woodrow Wilson on December 28, 1918, said: "The peoples of the world want peace and they want it now, not merely by conquest of arms, but by agreement of mind."

And Dwight D. Eisenhower, twenty-seven years later on July 12, 1945, said: "To preserve his freedom of worship, his equality before the law, his liberty to speak and act as he sees fit subject only to provisions that he trespass not upon similar rights of others, a Londoner will fight. So will a citizen of Abilene."

As we continue to work together, let us always remember that those few things that might divide us are as nothing compared to the great principles and policies which unite the free world.

Together let us work for this future, pledging to the world peace and justice, prosperity and trade, all achieved in a political climate that honors the ideals of freedom and the dignity of man.

1. *The Soviet Challenge* [3]

What must the United States do to meet the challenge to our national survival which is presented by the world Communist movement? I am not speaking now of the military challenge, although that is a very real one and I shall speak of it later. In the military area I am confident that the United States will do what is necessary to maintain the strength we need. The greater danger, in my view, is nonmilitary in character.

I will never forget what Mr. Khrushchev said to me in Moscow when we first met. As he looked over the wonderful exhibits we had at the American Exhibition there, he said something like this: "Mr. Vice President, you're ahead of us now economically, but we're moving faster than you are, our system is better than yours, and we're going to pass you by pretty soon, and we're going to wave to you as we go by and then we're going to say 'Come on, follow us and do as we do so that you don't fall behind any farther.'" That is what he

[3] The material in this section is derived from the following sources: Remarks at the 1960 Founders' Day Program, University of Nebraska, Lincoln, Nebraska. March 28, 1960. Remarks at Chicago "Dinner with Ike," Chicago, Illinois. January 27, 1960. Remarks at the University of Chicago Law School Center Dedication Ceremonies, Chicago, Illinois. October 5, 1959. Remarks to the American Society of Newspaper Editors, Washington, D.C. April 18, 1959. "Price Stability and Economic Growth," Address to Economic Conference, Washington, D.C. November 2, 1959. Responses to questions at the program of the Detroit Committee for Seven Eastern Women's Colleges, Inc., Detroit, Michigan. February 15, 1960. Responses to questions at the California Newspaper Publishers Association Convention, Los Angeles, California. February 6, 1960. Responses to questions at Conference with Representatives of the Four Armed Services, Washington, D.C. July 29, 1957. Remarks before the Convention of the National Council of Catholic Youth, Philadelphia, Pennsylvania. November 24, 1957. Remarks at the Annual Meeting of the National Association of Manufacturers, New York, New York. December 6, 1957.

said, and, what is more important, that is what he believes. In other words, he has boldly challenged the United States to competition. And he says the Communist system of slavery will outproduce the American system of freedom.

He put it very well, I think, from his standpoint when he was in New Delhi a few months ago. He likened the contest between our two systems to a horse race. Our system was one horse and the Communist system was another. And he said, "The horse you are riding in the United States is an old horse. It was a fine horse at one time, but now it's old and worn out and beginning to go lame. But the horse we're riding, our Communist horse, is young and vigorous and spirited, and we're going to pass you and win this race."

He left no doubt whatever of the massiveness and serious-ness of his challenge to our way of life. While he now rules out the use of force as an instrument of international policy, he reiterates again and again his faith that the United States and other free countries are destined eventually to come under Communist domination. In its simplest terms, his challenge is: let us have peaceful competition, communism against capi-talism, his system against ours. And he leaves no doubt about his faith as to the outcome: communism will inevitably prevail.

What should our answer be?

We should make it clear at the outset that we welcome competition. After all, competition is our idea. It is the mo-tivating drive responsible for the economic, political, and cul-tural progress of this nation. We are glad that Mr. Khrushchev recognizes its merits, and we welcome his challenge.

But we say, extend this competition to include the spiritual as well as the material aspects of our civilization. Let us com-pete in seeing who can produce a better life not only in terms of shelter, food, and clothing, but in terms of human freedom and individual dignity.

Can we win in this competition? The answer is yes, if we recognize some basic factors.

We must avoid at all costs any overconfidence just because the Communist idea is repugnant to us or because of our belief that the Communist system has built-in weaknesses which will eventually bring about its downfall.

We must always remember that a totalitarian system, in the short run, can concentrate immense power on chosen objectives; that the Russian people are working long and hard, driven by fanatically dedicated leaders who are motivated by but a single objective—the communization of the world; that the leaders as well as the people have a highly developed competitive spirit and that they have the advantage of anyone who is running behind in a race—the stimulus of trying to catch up and pass the front runner.

We can win in this competition, in other words, if we recognize their strength and if we work harder, believe more deeply, and are motivated by an even stronger competitive spirit than theirs.

But in recognizing the seriousness of their challenge, we could make no greater mistake than to go to the extreme of judging American institutions by the Communist yardstick.

I realize that there are many who complain that the Communists have a sense of purpose which we lack. And there is no question but that they do have a sense of purpose—that of imposing the Communist system on all the nations of the world.

In 1917 there were but 80,000 Communists in Czarist Russia. Not one government in the world was under Communist domination. By 1957, just forty years later, one billion people and twelve formerly independent nations were under the domination of the Communist government of the Soviet Union. Within the Soviet Union these positive results had been accomplished:

1. The weak, obsolete military establishment of the Russia of 1917 had been transformed into one of the most powerful military machines in world history.

2. A backward, primarily agricultural economy had been

replaced by a modern industrial plant in which steel production was 12 times as much, petroleum 11 times as much, coal 16 times as much, and electric power 111 times as much as it had been in 1917.

3. Russian science moved from the eighteenth to the twentieth century in the space of those forty years.

These things were not accomplished without great cost. On the debit side we find:

1. The standard of living of the average Russian not only has not kept pace with the rate of improvement in the free world, but actually is little better today than it was in 1917.

2. The income of the average Russian industrial worker in 1957 was only two-tenths of 1 per cent higher than it was in 1917. In that same period the income of the average American industrial worker went up 484 per cent.

3. The average Russian has poorer housing and poorer food than he did before the Bolshevik Revolution. Except for the elite few of the privileged class, Russia today is a gigantic poorhouse by free world standards, just as it was in 1917.

In summary: the Communist system has been good for the state and bad for the people.

There have been human costs also—more difficult to measure but even more significant in character. Twelve proud nations have lost their independence. Countless millions guilty only of opposition to the Communist regime have been sacrificed on the altar of the new class. The priceless freedoms we cherish have become casualties of Communist conquest.

When Mr. Mikoyan was here, I asked him, first before he started his swing around the United States, and again after he had visited Detroit, Los Angeles, and other great production centers of this country—after he had had an opportunity to see the conditions of our workers and our high living standards—how he thought communism would come to the United States. In presenting the question to him I said:

"In view of the standard of living of America's workers, in view of what our labor leaders have told you while you were here, do you believe that communism will come to the United States in the usual Marxist pattern of the workers rising against the bourgeoisie, or the employers, and establishing a government by the proletariat?"

His answer was very interesting. He said: "No, I will have to admit that the condition of your workers in the United States is such that we cannot rely on that method of bringing about communism. But of this I am sure: communism will eventually come to this country, and it will come in this way. It will come when the people of the United States will look at the Soviet Union and will see that our system is more productive, more efficient, and does more for people than yours. Then the people of the United States will turn to communism in order to avoid becoming a second-class power, economically."

Mr. Khrushchev, of course, would support Mr. Mikoyan in that view. And I would say the essential lesson for us is not that they said it, but that they believe it.

We must recognize that these Communist leaders who confront us, whatever we may think of them, have faith in their system. It follows that we need a similar faith, a faith in the fact that this system in our country and in other parts of the free world, with all its faults, has still produced the greatest prosperity, the greatest freedom, that men have ever known.

It is not enough for us to be on the right side. History is full of instances in which superior civilizations were overwhelmed by others with more will to win, more drive, more energy. Around the world, in every nation, the representatives of communism are true believers like Mr. Khrushchev—working overtime for the victory of communism in every non-Communist nation.

The fact that we have no desire to conquer the world does not mean that our alternative to communism is simply to leave the world as it is—ignoring the misery, disease, and inequity on which communism thrives. We, too, have a purpose and a mission in the world today—and that is what we must make clear as we meet the Communist challenge.

We offer our partnership, our advice and assistance, in helping peoples everywhere to achieve the economic progress which is essential if they are to have better food and housing and health than they presently enjoy.

But we do not stop here. We insist that man needs freedom —freedom of inquiry and information, freedom to seek knowledge, to express his views, freedom to choose his own leaders and hold them strictly accountable, freedom to shape his own destiny—and freedom to worship God in the light of his own conscience.

Our mission in the world today must be to extend to all mankind not just the ideal but the fact of freedom—by preserving and protecting and defending it, by helping others achieve it, by offering our own example of a free society at work.

From time to time, one hears the suggestion that fundamental changes are occurring within the Soviet Union, and that a system more congenial to the United States will soon emerge.

If the term "fundamental" refers to changes in the methods of production—agricultural production, for example, and the handling of the industrial economy—we could say there are fundamental changes taking place. On economic grounds it would not be inaccurate at the present time to call the competition between the U.S.S.R. and the United States a contest between two forms of capitalism—one controlled by the state, the other controlled by the independent, free market decisions and choices of literally millions of individuals—rather than between communism in the classic sense and free enterprise.

However, if when we speak of "fundamental" changes, we mean changes in the form of government, changes in the aim of the Soviet empire, as it were, I would say that such expectations are unrealistic.

Today the system of government in the Soviet Union is the same as the Communists inaugurated when they first came to power. It is a system in which a small group of men dominate the whole society industrially, economically, and politically. Moreover, the system of government in the Soviet Union still has as its object not only continued domination over its own people, but eventual world domination—by war if necessary, by other means if possible.

Under these circumstances, we would be making a great error if we believed that those changes that do take place—in the Soviet hierarchy, for example, in the economy, in production methods and the like—imply any fundamental change in the Soviet system as such.

Similarly, it is often suggested that revolution, and not evolution or external war, will bring about the speedy downfall of the Soviet system. I would hesitate to comment on such expectations categorically. I remember that in World War II, or immediately before, many people said that eventually Hitler would be overthrown by revolution. There were those who categorically said it would not happen and those who said it would. Eventually, of course, Hitler fell, essentially as a result of force from without but perhaps from some decay from within as well.

With regard to the Communist system, and in view of what happened in Hungary, we certainly cannot rule out the possibility of revolt. Yet, from all the reports I have been able to read, intelligence and otherwise, the present leadership still exercises iron control over the Soviet empire and is likely to maintain it for some years to come. We cannot base our policy on the possibility that revolt may come in the near future.

How, then, do we meet Khrushchev's economic challenge?

We have heard a lot about the things that are wrong with the American economy—and certainly it is not perfect. But let's look at some of the things that are right about this American economy that the Communists and many domestic critics say is fat and complacent and stagnant. Let's set the record straight.

This "stagnant" economy of ours today produces more jobs for more people at higher wages than has that of any other nation in the history of the world. In America today, more individuals own their own homes, drive their own cars, hold shares in business and industry than ever before in this country or any other. We are ahead of the Soviet Union in the production of every major industrial product. Our total production is more than double theirs by any standards. And as I said to Mr. Khrushchev in Moscow: "We in the United States have achieved in great measure the economic objective of abundance for all in a classless society that Communist theory merely promises."

Now this is no cause for complacency. The Communists are working hard, they are being driven at a fanatical pace, and despite the inherent deficiencies in their system, they present a real challenge to us. But there is no reason for lack of confidence in our ability to stay ahead in this "horse race," provided we remain true to our basic principles—provided, so to speak, we stay on our horse and do not try to get on theirs.

Perhaps the best way that we can illustrate this point of our staying on our own horse is to refer to an attitude which is quite common, among the unsophisticated, when such problems as inflation and economic growth are discussed. It is often expressed somewhat along these lines: why doesn't the government do something to stop inflation? Why doesn't the government do something to assure economic growth?

Everybody is against inflation, or at least presumably should be, and everybody is for economic growth. The question is, who has the primary responsibility to do something about it? And all too often the assumption is: "Why, those people in

Washington, of course; they and they alone are the ones who can adopt policies which will make sure that the dollar is sound, that there is no inflation. Why don't they do it? And as far as economic growth is concerned, if we have growth, it is going to come by reason of what Washington does, almost exclusively."

As we consider this judgment we should recognize that it would be a very reasonable approach—if we were living in a totalitarian society. If such were the case, we could properly say that the sole responsibility for growth, and the responsibility for stability in prices, would rest squarely with those who ran the economy, the select few at the top who made the basic economic decisions. In the Soviet Union, Mr. Khrushchev and his colleagues have that responsibility. If growth comes, they get the credit. If it does not come, theirs is the blame for having failed to adopt policies that would have assured it.

And this brings us to the key question. Is it possible for a system like ours, a free society, to compete effectively with a totalitarian society—one in which a few men at the top can make decisions, choose the targets on which they are going to concentrate, and then provide the necessary resources to reach their goals? In view of recent developments, not only the Sputniks but other developments in the field of outer space, and in view of the general claims of progress that have been made by the Soviet Union, and the tremendously high goals for growth (7, 8, 9, and 10 per cent per year) which they have set for themselves—in view of all these things, is it possible that we may be on the wrong track? Is it possible that we should, in analyzing our own system, find ways and means of giving more power to government; more power to assure price stability, which is a sound foundation for economic growth; more power to stimulate production and place the resources of the country, human and material, into those areas which will best serve the national interest?

Before jumping to any such conclusion, it is important to analyze what has happened in the totalitarian economies, and particularly within the Soviet Union itself. It is very dangerous to oversimplify complicated economic questions, but based on my own rather brief travels in the Soviet Union, and also on my studies of the reports of others who have looked into economic conditions there, I think certain observations can be made. First, as far as their growth is concerned, it has been considerable. Of course, the fact that they started from a much lower base accounts for the *rate* of growth to some extent. We can point to the fact, for example, that the Canadians, starting from almost as low a base, have had growth patterns which are at least comparable to Russia's. Such things as these should be stressed to put in proper perspective the rate of growth of the Soviet Union from 1917 up to this point. On the other hand, if we are going to be objective (which we will have to be to survive in this world) we must agree that they have made great general progress. Furthermore, their totalitarian system allows them to concentrate their efforts in one area and achieve massive "break-throughs," as they have in the field of space exploration.

However, when we look a little deeper we find that the people in their industries, their mines, their factories, even on their farms, and especially in the scientific areas—that the people in the Communist empire (particularly is this true in the Soviet Union), in order to get production moving, have had to depart from Communist principles. For example, in factory after factory that I visited I found that the differential between those who were the top producers, the best thinkers, the most creative contributors, on the one hand, and the average worker, on the other, was far greater in the Soviet Union than in the United States, or in any other capitalist country in the world today. I found that the rewards which are given to scientists and to engineers are relatively greater than they are in a country like the United States. I found that they have abandoned the system by which everybody produces according to his ability and receives according to his needs. The way they are improving production is by departing radically from Communist principles. Competition is such that in a twenty-four-hour work day each eight-hour shift competes against the other two to see which can produce the most. This is the kind of device that the Soviet Union is using to get the most "forced draft" growth. And we find too that among the incentives they are turning to are rewards like owning a little piece of private property, and, in some instances, even having what is a kind of bank account.

In summary, you find in the Soviet Union today this significant fact: one of the reasons they are making economic progress is that they are turning our way. The lesson for us is that the greatest mistake we could make at a time when they are turning our way would be for us to turn their way.

Now let me develop this just a little further. How can we—in a free society, where government cannot and should not make absolute decisions that will assure price stability and economic growth—how can we effectively meet the challenge of a totalitarian economy?

First of all, I think we have already pointed up one very definite principle: price stability and economic growth are the government's business, but government cannot do the job alone. Price stability and economic growth are everybody's business in a free economy. The people themselves must support sound economic policies if we are to avoid ever greater inflationary pressures. The men in the Senate and the House (and I have served in both of these bodies) are, we can be sure, people of ability and character. But they cannot, over a period of time, stand for and vote for policies which the people back home will not support.

In addition, it is not only what government does that is important. What is done by all segments of the private sector of the economy is vitally important. The wage policies of labor, the private policies of management, the policies of our farmers, our veterans, and all the other groups in the economy—all these are tremendously important. Unless the whole economic complex joins together in an assault on this problem, we are not going to be able to meet and deal with it effectively.

Americans must understand that a government cannot consistently spend more than it takes in without running the risk of debasing its currency. We must also understand that the way to growth is not simply by having the Federal government spend more. The way we have had great growth in the past is by expanding the private sector of the economy, not the government sector. In this connection I might make this one observation. In contrasting "economic conservatives" with "economic liberals" (or whatever term you would like to apply to those who do not follow the conservative line), the problem is generally that, while the conservative policies work better, they are much more difficult to understand and much more difficult to sell. It is easy to attribute to government the responsibility for keeping prices stable and for producing growth. It is much more difficult to understand that, while governmental policies can create a *climate* for growth, the direct responsibility for growth is primarily on the private sector of the economy; and that the way to stimulate growth is not by increasing the government's participation in the economy, but by increasing the contributions that individuals, working cooperatively and by themselves, can and will make.

We cannot consider our economy in negative "stand-pat" terms. Inflation is bad. But we must not think only in terms of controlling inflation, maintaining price stability, keeping what we have. We must not strive for price stability or inflation control as an end in itself, but as a means to dynamic, sound economic growth—the kind of growth that will enable the United States, with its free economy, to outproduce the Communist economy of the Soviet Union or of any other potential opponent the United States may have.

But we could make no greater mistake than to attempt to meet Communist competition merely on the grounds they select. We are convinced that our system is more efficient and more productive than the Communist system. But we have far more to offer than an abundant production of material goods. The answer to atheistic Communist materialism is not just more and better materialism. They offer progress at the cost of freedom. Our alternative is progress *with* freedom—and, in fact, progress *because of* freedom.

The march of civilization cannot and must not be confined merely to economic systems. That is why Mr. Khrushchev's so-called historical analysis in which he traces a line of progress from feudalism to capitalism to communism falls down. History cannot be judged solely in material and economic terms. When we analyze these three systems in terms of freedom for the individual, we find that the change from feudalism to private capitalism was one from less freedom to more freedom. And a change now to communism would be going back rather than forward—exactly the reverse of progress.

That is why we say, let us broaden this competition to include the higher cultural and spiritual values that characterize the true forward march of our civilization. We reject the idea that the goals and desires of mankind begin and end with material abundance. Our homes, our highways, our motorcars and electronic marvels are not ends in themselves but only the means, the necessary foundations for a life of cultural and spiritual richness. For us this must be a life of individual freedom and human dignity, a life that liberates the human spirit of every restraint beyond its own inherent capability—and then goes on to expand and increase that capability.

In this peaceful competition, therefore, let us test our systems to see which provides for individual human beings the greater opportunities for personal freedom and personal expression. Our mission must not be simply the negative objective of the defeat of communism, but the positive goal of victory. And the victory we work for is not the victory of America over any other people, but the victory of all mankind— the victory of knowledge over ignorance, of plenty over want, of health over disease, of freedom and justice over tyranny, wherever these evils may exist in the world.

2. *Khrushchev in America* [4]

I believe the decision to invite Mr. Khrushchev to come to the United States was correct. In indicating my reasons for reaching this conclusion, let me first remind you of the background from which I speak. I have made a comprehensive study of the philosophy, tactics, and strategy of communism as set forth by Marx, Lenin, Stalin, and other Communist leaders. On the basis of these studies, I know that Communists throughout the world are united in working for one objective—Communist rule over all the people of the world.

I know from experience that the Communist Party in the United States, like all Communist Parties throughout the world, is directed and controlled from Moscow and has in the past and will in the future engage in espionage and subversion in order to serve the interests of Communist governments wherever they are opposed to those of the United States or other free nations. And I can vividly recall that not so long ago

[4] The material in this section is derived from the following sources:

Remarks before the Forty-first National Convention of the American Legion, Minneapolis, Minnesota. August 25, 1959. Remarks at the University of Chicago Law School Center Dedication Ceremonies, Chicago, Illinois. October 5, 1959. Remarks at the Centennial Session of the American Dental Association, New York, New York, September 14, 1959.

Communist-led mobs made an unsuccessful attempt on my life in Venezuela.[5]

When I was in the Soviet Union I had the opportunity to speak at length with Mr. Khrushchev and to appraise the present tactics and strategy of the world Communist movement. On the basis of that visit I can say unequivocally that the only significant change in Communist tactics since the death of Stalin is that Mr. Khrushchev and other Communist leaders now say they will accomplish their objective of world domination without resort to war.

Subversion and espionage in the United States and other non-Communist countries continue to be directed and supported by the Communist Party of the U.S.S.R. The positions of the Soviet government on such key issues as Berlin, disarmament, setting up an inspection system for prevention of surprise attack, and ending atomic tests are essentially the same now as they were before these visits were announced. Communist tactics constantly shift—but the major strategic goals remain the same.

It would be naïve and wishful thinking to assume that the visit of Mr. Khrushchev to the United States will result in any basic change in the Communist objective of world domination or their adherence to policies designed to achieve that goal.

We should be under no illusions that Mr. Khrushchev's belief in the superiority of the Communist system will be changed in any significant respect by his seeing the great productivity of the American economy. He is, to use his own words, a "hopeless" Communist. Everything he sees in the United States will be seen through Communist eyes, and the picture will be distorted or magnified so that it fits into the

---

[5] For an account of the Vice President's Latin American trip in the spring of 1958—during which his life was threatened by Communist-inspired mobs in both Caracas, Venezuela, and Lima, Peru—and for his subsequent policy-recommendations, see below Part III, Section 4 (Foreign Policy in Action: Latin America), pp. 91ff.

rigid description of free societies which Communist doctrine has painted for over 100 years.

Nor should we be under any illusions that better understanding between the Soviet leaders and ourselves is all that is needed to resolve our differences and to assure peace. There are some deep and basic conflicts of interest and ideology which all the good will and mutual understanding in the world will not settle. Charm, words of friendship, gracious toasts are not going to have the slightest effect in deterring Mr. Khrushchev from his basic objectives.

What useful purpose, then, will this visit serve? Putting it in its simplest terms, while understanding alone will not bring peace, misunderstanding—and sheer misinformation, sheer ignorance—could provoke war. And it is because his visit can serve to reduce the possibilities of such misunderstanding that it could contribute to the chance that we can settle our differences without war and, therefore, deserves the approval of the American people.

What manner of man is this Russian leader? Based on my conversations with him and my analysis of the statements he has made, publicly and privately, through the years, here is a thumbnail sketch of the man who, by his decision alone, could start a chain reaction that would destroy civilization as we know it.

I was especially impressed, when I met him, with his tremendous vitality and physical energy. His mental reactions are keen and quick. He is aggressive and resourceful in debate —always on the offensive. He is an uninhibited extrovert with a rare gift for interpolating salty statements and humorous anecdotes into his speeches and conversations. If my own experience is any guide, there is never a dull moment when he is around!

In my discussions with him in Moscow he said: "You, Mr. Vice President, are a lawyer for capitalism and I am a lawyer for communism; and even though I have no legal training I don't intend to let down the workers whom I represent." I would have to concede that no one could have been more relentless in presenting what we believe to be a bad case.

While at times he may appear to be emotional and impetuous, I found that in private conversation when the chips were down he was a calculating, tough-minded advocate of his point of view. In one sense, this cold realism of his is a good thing. The more realistic Khrushchev remains, the less likely it is that by simple miscalculation he may be led into indiscretions and overenthusiasm that might precipitate war.

In appraising his over-all ability, I recall a very revealing conversation I had with a European diplomat shortly after Mr. Khrushchev came to power. At that time, after his first visit to Yugoslavia, there were some observers who tended to write him off as an emotionally unstable, uneducated individual who would not be able to hold his own in world councils. My friend told me that, in his opinion, it was a grave error to draw this conclusion. He said: "Anyone who has fought his way up through the jungle warfare of the Communist hierarchy until he reached the top of the heap, and has survived forty years of purges, intrigue, and plotting, simply has to be a man to reckon with." I think most of us would agree that this analysis has proved to be correct.

He has more uncontrolled power in his hands than any leader in the history of the world. This does not mean that he does not consult with others in his government. But all of those who have participated in conferences with him—where men like Mr. Mikoyan and Mr. Kozlov have also been present—have noted, as I did, that Mr. Khrushchev does all the talking that amounts to anything. Mr. Mikoyan and Mr. Kozlov were there not to advise him but to agree with him.

What does Mr. Khrushchev really believe about the United States and the free world?

First, here are some things he believes which are true. He is aware of the fact that the United States has great military strength. While he constantly boasts of his superiority in the missile field, he has publicly stated in a speech at Dnepropetrovsk on July 28, 1959, that no nation today can initiate a war without suffering terrible destruction in return.

He knows the United States is a rich country with a high standard of living. He has paid us the compliment of setting as the Soviet goal catching up with and passing the United States in the production of consumer goods.

I believe he is convinced that President Eisenhower is a man who wants peace and who insists that the United States remain strong only because he believes this is the way to keep peace. But he also has some dangerous misconceptions about the United States and the free world which, in the mind of a man with such awesome power in his hands, constitute a terrible risk to the peace of the world.

Here are some of the things he presently believes about us and our policies:

"Freedom in the United States exists only for those who have money and power and not for the working people."

"Capitalists in the United States have turned the society which they rule into a paradise for the rich and a hell for the poor—a kingdom of the dollar, of harsh exploitation of millions of people to enrich a handful of monopolists."

"In the United States and other free countries the working people are given the right to vote for various representatives of the ruling class but have no right to participate in the work of the legislative bodies."

"However beautifully the ideologists of imperialism may dress up the capitalist system, it still remains a system by which millions of people are enslaved by a comparatively small handful of exploiters, a system in which poverty and mass unemployment reign."

The words I have just quoted are not mine but his—taken

directly from his public statements—and these ideas he re-iterated to me in my conversations with him. Because he believes these things he has reached other conclusions which he has stated to me and to others who have talked with him: that millions of people in the United States do not support the President in his firm stand against Communist aggression; that both of our major political parties are controlled by a few rich monopolists and are not responsive to the will of the people; that our economy has reached its peak and is on the way down; that the nations of the free world alliance are divided and, when the chips are down, will not unite in resisting aggression.

Put yourself in his place. If you possessed great military strength with uncontrolled and absolute power to use that strength to accomplish your purposes; if also you were fanatically dedicated to the philosophy that your economic and political system would and should rule the world; and if in addition you believed you were confronted by opponents who were divided and who lacked the will to resist aggression—would you not be tempted to be far more aggressive in your policies than if you had other ideas as to the strength and will to resist of those who might oppose your aims?

I have seen and talked to Mr. Khrushchev. I am convinced that if he continues to believe what he presently believes about us we can only expect him to continue on his present course of reckless unilateral action like his precipitation of the Berlin crisis. And the consequences could be a war that would destroy civilization itself.

Will Mr. Khrushchev's visit to the United States change his views significantly? As a Communist he will not and cannot admit that the Communist predictions with regard to the eventual collapse of capitalism are being proved false in this country.

But we should not overlook another characteristic of Mr. Khrushchev which I noted time after time in my talks with him. While he is badly misinformed about life in the United States, he is an intensely pragmatic and curious man who likes to see for himself. And he believes what he sees far more than what he hears.

Mr. Khrushchev will be here for only a relatively brief time, but, in his conversations with President Eisenhower and in his trip across the country, there is no doubt in my mind but that he will see and hear some things which will change his preconceived notions about the United States and which, in turn, will give him pause before he embarks on a course of action in the future which might be contrary to our vital interests.

He will find not only that we are strong militarily and economically, but that the American people have the will to use their strength to defend their freedom or the freedom of others any place in the world. He will find that the overwhelming majority of the American people are as dedicated to their system as he is to his. He will find that we will no more tolerate being pushed around than he will.

The peace we want is not the peace of surrender or appeasement: it is peace with justice. If Mr. Khrushchev has this lesson brought home to him by what he sees and hears in the United States, this visit will have been justified—apart from the results of any conversations he may have with the President—because it will have reduced the possibility that he may underestimate our will to resist and thereby precipitate a crisis which could only result in war.

If a man is to have such awesome power as Mr. Khrushchev possesses, it is far better that he base his decisions on firsthand knowledge of the United States and its strength rather than on secondhand reports which must be filtered through the wall of secrecy and suspicion that surrounds the Kremlin.

In addition to giving Mr. Khrushchev a chance to see the United States and to know the truth about the American people, his visit will provide an opportunity for him to discuss directly with President Eisenhower issues that affect the peace of the world.

Now I realize that there are those who object to such talks on the ground that they may result in appeasement, the surrender of some of our basic interests; some even suggest that Mr. Khrushchev may outwit, outsmart, or trap the President and his associates. I think it is time for us to recognize that the Communists are not so smart and we are not so dumb as such suggestions would imply.

In the past the difficulty has been not what was agreed upon at the conference table but the fact that the Communists broke the agreements. This has occurred in the case of fifty out of fifty-two major treaties and agreements since 1933.

We can be sure that the President will have in mind the 1955 Geneva Conference, for example, where Mr. Khrushchev made agreements on the unification of Germany and other issues which to date he has failed to carry out. The President is well aware that Communist subversion in the United States is still being financed and supported by the Communist Party of the Soviet Union. And if there was ever any doubt that the President would enter these talks with his guard up, the news from Laos has certainly laid them to rest. The support and the encouragement which the governments of the U.S.S.R. and Communist China have been giving to the rebels in that country—including equipment and even staging areas—have served to alert the whole free world to the fact that communism's drive for world domination continues without letup.

Let me list some of the things that will *not* result from Mr. Khrushchev's visit.

There will be no acquiescence or approval by us of the status of the captive nations of Eastern Europe. There will be no change in the opposition of the government and people of the United States to communism at home or abroad. There will be no reduction of United States military strength in the absence of self-enforcing disarmament agreements which we know will be kept by the U.S.S.R. as well as by us. There will, in view of their absence, be no negotiating on issues affecting our allies. And there will be no abandonment of our position that the 2½ million people of West Berlin must continue to retain the free government which they have chosen by overwhelming vote.

In other words, those who believe that this conference is going to result in appeasement, surrender, defensiveness, and softness toward communism simply do not know the President of the United States.

We have learned a lot in our dealings with the Communists over the past few years. While we will always treat a guest in our country with courtesy, we know that flattery and toasts have no effect whatever in changing the rigid positions of the Communist leaders. We have learned that in our meetings with them we have to be just as hardheaded, tough-minded, and realistic as they are. This is an approach Mr. Khrushchev respects and understands, and this is the approach President Eisenhower will take.

There are some who say it was undignified for me to reply to Mr. Khrushchev in public when he attacked the United States and our policies when I was escorting him through the United States Exhibition in Moscow.

My answer is that I, too, would prefer that important issues be discussed in a dignified private conference. But what we have to recognize is that we are engaged in a great battle of ideas with the Communist world. Mr. Khrushchev knows this well. He never misses an opportunity to make propaganda for the Communist way of life. And I say that we in the free world must not be defensive or apologetic when our system comes under attack, publicly or privately. We must stand up and fight for our ideas just as the Communists do for theirs. Too often we have allowed to go unchallenged such talk as: the free nations are decadent, divided, and weak; the only and best way to progress in the newly developing countries is through communism; communism rather than freedom is the wave of the future; the Communist leaders are too crafty and shrewd for us at the conference table; their educational system is superior to ours.

We have been on the defensive long enough. It is time for us to take the offensive and help make the whole world realize that the Communist idea is not a super-idea; that the Communist leaders are not supermen; and that the Soviet Union is not a super-nation.

I do not mean that we should underestimate the deadly seriousness of the challenge which is presented to us because of the disciplined dedication of the Communist leaders. But let us not make the mistake of meeting that challenge with a negative, defeatist, static posture. As the international spotlight shifts from long-distance threats to man-to-man conferences, we should be cautious. But caution is not the same as a paralyzing suspicion that prevents any move toward peace.

When Mr. Khrushchev challenges us to peaceful competition, let us go him one better and urge expansion of that competition to include the spiritual as well as the material aspects of our society. Let there be competition between ideas not only in the free world but in the Communist world as well—and between the two.

We should welcome and encourage a greater exchange of persons and ideas between the free world and the Communist world. A free society thrives on discussion, criticism, and interplay of ideas. On the other hand, dictators use fear, suspicion, and secrecy to maintain their power and control over the people.

When Mr. Khrushchev says that our grandchildren will live under communism, our answer should be: we do not fear the outcome, provided they have the freedom to choose the system they want. We do not say in reply that his grandchildren will

live under capitalism. The very essence of our belief is that
we will not impose it on anyone else; every nation should
have the right to choose—free of any outside interference—the
kind of economic and political system which best fits its
particular problems.

But this we do believe: that all the people on this earth,
including those in the Soviet Union, will inevitably demand
and obtain more and more freedom. Because history teaches
us that man was made to be free and that freedom, not
communism or any other form of dictatorship, is the wave of
the future.

The best answer to the Communist Revolution is the kind
of life produced by the American Revolution. The most effective antidote to communism is a program of intelligent, articulate, positive Americanism.

PART THREE

U.S. Foreign Policy:
Peace with Freedom
and Justice

1. *The Rule of Law* [6]

The most difficult problem confronting our society today is, as I am sure we all agree, the simple but overriding question of the survival of our civilization. While none of us would downgrade the importance of such challenging problems as the control of inflation, economic growth, civil rights, or urban redevelopment, we all know that the most perfect solutions of any of our domestic problems will make no difference at all if we are not around to enjoy them.

Perhaps at no time in the course of history have so many people been so sorely troubled by the problems of the times and dismayed by the prospects of the future. The almost unbelievably destructive power of modern weapons should be enough to raise grave doubts as to mankind's ability to survive, even were we living in a world in which traditional patterns of international conduct were being followed by the major nations. But the threat to our survival is frighteningly multiplied when we take into account the fact that these weapons are in the hands of the unpredictable leaders of the Communist world as well as those of the free world.

What is the way out of this twentieth-century dilemma?

We can take confidence in the fact that at this moment the United States possesses military power fully adequate to sustain its policies, and I am certain that whatever is necessary to keep this balance in favor of the free nations will be done— by this Administration and by its successors, regardless of which political party may be in power.

What this posture of resolute national unity, taken alone,

[6] The material in this section is derived from an Address before the Academy of Political Science, New York, New York. April 13, 1959.

must mean in the end, however, is simply an indefinite preservation of the balance of terror.

We all recognize that this is not enough. Even though our dedication to strength will reduce sharply the chances of war by deliberate overt act, as long as the rule of force retains its paramount position as the final arbiter of international disputes there will still remain the possibility of war by miscalculation. If this sword of annihilation is ever to be removed from its precarious balance over the head of all mankind, some more positive courses of action than massive military deterrence must somehow be found.

It is an understandable temptation for men in public life to suggest that some bold new program will resolve the human dilemma—that more missiles, more aid, more trade, more exchange, or more meetings at the summit will magically solve the world's difficulties.

The proposals that I will suggest here are not offered as a panacea for the world's ills. In fact, to suggest that any one program, whatever its merits, can automatically solve the world's problems is not only unrealistic but—considering the kind of opponent who faces us across the world today—actually can do more harm than good. It tends to minimize the scope and gravity of the problems with which we are confronted, by suggesting that there may be one easy answer.

But while there is no simple solution for the problems we face, we must constantly search for new practical alternatives to the use of force as a means of settling disputes between nations.

Men face essentially similar problems of disagreement and resort to force in their personal and community lives as nations now do in the divided world. And, historically, man has found only one effective way to cope with this aspect of human nature—the rule of law.

More and more the leaders of the West have come to the conclusion that the rule of law must somehow be established to provide a way of settling disputes among nations as it does among individuals. But the trouble has been that as yet we have been unable to find practical methods of implementing this idea. Is this one of those things that men can think about but never quite achieve?

Let us see what a man who had one of the most brilliant political and legal minds in the nation's history had to say in this regard. Commenting on some of the problems of international organization, the late Senator Robert Taft said: "I do not see how we can hope to secure permanent peace in the world except by establishing law between nations and equal justice under law. It may be a long hard course but I believe that the public opinion of the world can be led along that course, so that the time will come when that public opinion will support the decision of any reasonable impartial tribunal based on justice."

We can also be encouraged by developments that have occurred in this field in just the past few years.

Not surprisingly, the movement to advance the rule of law has gained most of its momentum among lawyers. Mr. Charles Rhyne, a recent President of the American Bar Association, declared in a speech in 1959 that there is "an idea on the march" in the world. He was referring to the idea that ultimately the rule of law must replace the balance of terror as the paramount factor in the affairs of men.

At the time of the grand meeting of the American Bar Association in London in July, 1957, speaker after speaker—the Chief Justice of the United States, the Lord Chancellor of Great Britain, the Attorney General of the United States, and Sir Winston Churchill—eloquently testified that law must be made paramount in world affairs.

An adviser to the President, Mr. Arthur Larson, left the White House staff in 1958 to establish a World Rule of Law Center at Duke University.

One-hundred and eighty-five representatives of the legal

professions of many nations of the earth met in New Delhi in January, 1958, and agreed that there are basic universal principles on which lawyers of the free world can agree.

In 1958, through the activity of the Bar Association and by proclamation of the President, May 1—the Communist May Day—became Law Day in the United States. The Bar Association stimulated more than 20,000 meetings over the country on the first Law Day. Each year this tribute to an advancing idea is repeated on an ever greater scale.

President Eisenhower, you will recall, said in his State of the Union Message in January, 1959: "It is my purpose to intensify efforts during the coming two years—to the end that the rule of law may replace the obsolete rule of force in the affairs of nations. Measures toward this end will be proposed later, including reexamination of our relation to the International Court of Justice."

I am now convinced, and in this I reflect the steadfast purpose of the President, and the wholehearted support of the Secretary of State and the Attorney General, that the time has come to take the initiative in the direction of establishment of the rule of law in the world to replace the rule of force.

Under the Charter of the United Nations and the Statute of the International Court of Justice, institutions for the peaceful composing of differences among nations and for lawgiving exist in the international community. Our primary problem today is not the creation of new international institutions, but the fuller and more fruitful use of the institutions we already possess.

The International Court of Justice is a case in point. Its relative lack of judicial business—in its fourteen-year history an average of only two cases a year have come before this tribunal of fifteen outstanding international jurists—underlines the untried potentialities of the Court. While it would be foolish to suppose that litigation before the Court is the answer to all the world's problems, this method of settling disputes could profitably be employed in a wider range of cases than is presently done.

As the President indicated, it is time for the United States to reexamine its own position with regard to the Court. Clearly, all disputes regarding domestic matters must remain permanently within the jurisdiction of our own courts. Only matters which are essentially international in character should be referred to the International Court. But the United States reserved the right to determine unilaterally whether the subject matter of a particular dispute is within the domestic jurisdiction of the United States and is therefore excluded from the jurisdiction of the Court. As a result of this position on our part, other nations have adopted similar reservations. This is one of the major reasons for the lack of judicial business before the Court.

To remedy this situation the Administration has submitted to the Congress recommendations for modifying this reservation.[7] It is our hope that by taking the initiative in this way, other countries may be persuaded to accept and agree to a wider jurisdiction of the International Court.

There is one class of disputes between nations—I refer to economic disputes—which, in the past, has been one of the primary causes of war. These economic disputes assume major importance today at a time when the cold war may be shifting its major front from politics and ideology to the so-called "ruble war" for the trade and the development of new and neutral countries.

[7] The President has recommended to the Senate (86th Congress, 2nd Session) that this reservation, the so-called Connally Amendment (originally proposed by the then-chairman of the Senate Foreign Relations Committee, Tom Connally of Texas), be abrogated. To date, the Foreign Relations Committee has made no report, favorable or unfavorable, to the full Senate; it seems nearly impossible, therefore, that the 86th Congress will take any action on this recommendation.

As far as international trade is concerned, an imposing structure of international agreements already exists. More complex and urgent than trade, as such, is the area of international investment. For in this area will be determined one of the most burning issues of our times—whether the economic development of new nations, so essential to their growth in political self-confidence and successful self-government, will be accomplished peacefully or violently, swiftly or wastefully, in freedom or in regimentation and terror.

We must begin by recognizing that the task of providing the necessary capital for investment in underdeveloped countries is a job too big for mere government money. Only private money, privately managed, can do the job as it should be done in many areas in need of development. And private investment requires a sound and reliable framework of laws in which to work.

Economic development, involving as it does so many lawyers and so many private investors, will tend to spread and promote more civilized legal systems wherever it goes. Already, in its effort to encourage private investment abroad, the United States government has negotiated treaties of commerce with seventeen nations since 1946, tax conventions with twenty-one nations, and special investment guaranty agreements under the Mutual Security Act with forty nations. A host of other special arrangements are in effect, such as those under which we have helped six nations draft better domestic legislation relating to foreign investment.

What has been done is for the most part good, but there are several areas where additional action is called for. The countries that need economic development most are too often least likely to have the kind of laws, government, and political climate that will attract investment. The political risks of expropriation and inconvertibility against which ICA presently sells insurance are not the only political risks that investors fear. Three United States government commissions, as well as numerous private experts, have recently recommended a variety of improvements in our machinery for fostering foreign investment.

I select three for particular endorsement. Our laws should permit the establishment of foreign business corporations meriting special tax treatment, so that their foreign earnings can be reinvested abroad free of United States tax until the investor actually receives his reward. In addition, more tax treaties should be speedily negotiated to permit "tax-sparing" and other reciprocal encouragements to investors. The ICA guaranty program should be extended to cover such risks as revolution and civil strife. Finally, a concerted effort should be made to extend our whole treaty and guaranty system into more countries, especially those most in need of development.

The great adventure of economic development through a worldwide expansion of private investment is bound to develop many new forms and channels of cooperation between governments and between individuals of different nations.

We need not fear this adventure; indeed, we should welcome it. For if it sufficiently engages the imagination and public spirit of the legal profession and others who influence public opinion, it must be accompanied by the discovery or rediscovery, in countries old and new, of the legal principles and the respect for substantive law on which wealth and freedom alike are grounded.

There are encouraging signs that we are at least on the threshold of real progress toward creating more effective international law for the settlement of economic disputes between individuals and between nations.

Turning to the political area, we have now come far enough along in the great historic conflict between the free nations and the Communist bloc to know that negotiation and discussion alone will not necessarily resolve the fundamental issues between us. This has proved to be the case whether the negotiations took place through the very helpful processes of the United Nations, or at the conference table of foreign ministers, or even at what we now call the summit.

What emerges, eventually, from these meetings at the conference table are agreements. We have made a great many agreements with the Soviet leaders from the time of Yalta and Potsdam. A major missing element in our agreements with the Soviet leaders has been any provision for deciding disputes about the meaning of the agreements in connection with their implementation.

Looking back at the 1955 Geneva Summit Conference, for example, we find that it produced an agreement, signed by the Soviet leaders, which elevated the hopes of the entire world.

It should be noted, however, that the President and the Secretary of State repeatedly warned both before and after the conference that success could be measured only in deeds. One of the announced purposes of the conference was to test Soviet sincerity by the only standard that counts in the long run—the standard of performance.

That Summit Conference was afterward characterized by some as a failure, but in terms of agreements, as such, it was a success.

Let me quote briefly from that agreement: "The heads of government, recognizing their common responsibility for the settlement of the German question and the reunification of Germany, have agreed that the settlement of the German question and the reunification of Germany by means of free elections shall be carried out in conformity with the national interests of the German people and the interest of European security."

In other words, those who participated in the conference, including Mr. Khrushchev, agreed at Geneva on a sound method for dealing with the German problem—the very same problem from which he later fathered new crises over Berlin.

But while the agreement seemed clear, as events subsequently developed, Mr. Khrushchev's understanding of its meaning was ostensibly different from ours.

The crucial question remained—how was the agreement to be effective when the parties disagreed as to what it meant? This is typical of a problem that can arise wherever any agreement is entered into between nations.

In looking to the future what practical steps can we take to meet this problem? I will not even suggest to you that there is any simple answer to this question, for obviously there can be none. But I do believe there is a significant step we can take toward finding an answer.

We should take the initiative in urging that in future agreements provisions be included to the effect that (1) disputes which may arise as to the interpretation of the agreement should be submitted to the International Court of Justice at The Hague; and (2) the nations signing the agreement be bound by the decision of the Court in such cases.

Such provisions will, of course, still leave us with many formidable questions involving our relationships with the Communist nations in those cases where they ignore an agreement completely apart from its interpretation. But I believe this would be a major step forward in developing a rule of law for the settlement of political disputes between nations and in the direction all free men hope to pursue. If there is no provision for settling disputes as to what an international agreement means, and if one nation is acting in bad faith, the agreement has relatively little significance. In the absence of such a provision, an agreement can be flagrantly nullified by a nation acting in bad faith whenever it determines it is convenient to do so.

While this proposal has not yet been adopted as the official United States position, I have discussed it at length with Attorney General Rogers and with officials of the State Department. And on the basis of these discussions I am convinced that it has merit and should be given serious consideration in the future.

The International Court of Justice is not a Western instrument. It is a duly constituted body under the United Nations Charter and has been recognized and established by the Soviet Union along with the other signatories of the Charter.

There is no valid reason why the Soviets should not be willing to join with the nations of the free world in taking this step in the direction of submitting differences with regard to interpretation of agreements between nations to a duly established international court and thereby further the day when the rule of law will become a reality in the relations between nations.

And, on our part, as Secretary Dulles said in his speech before the New York State Bar Association in January, 1959: "Those nations which do have common standards should, by their conduct and example, advance the rule of law by submitting their disputes to the International Court of Justice, or to some other international tribunal upon which they agree."

We should be prepared to show the world by our example that the rule of law, even in the most trying circumstances, is the one system which all free men of good will must support.

In this connection it should be noted that at the present time in our own country our system of law and justice has come under special scrutiny, as it often has before in periods when we have been engaged in working out basic social relationships through due process of law. It is certainly proper for any of us to disagree with an opinion of a court or courts. But all Americans owe it to the most fundamental propositions of our way of life to take the greatest care in making certain that our criticisms of court decisions do not become attacks on the institution of the court itself.

Mr. Khrushchev has proclaimed time and again that he and his associates in the Kremlin, to say nothing of the Soviet people, desire only a fair competition to test which system, communism or free capitalism, can better meet the legitimate aspirations of mankind for a rising standard of living.

Perhaps it is significant that the leaders of the free world do not feel obliged to so proclaim so often. The world knows that this is the only kind of competition which the free nations desire. It is axiomatic that free people do not go to war except in defense of freedom. So obviously we welcome this kind of talk from Mr. Khrushchev. We welcome a peaceful competition with the Communists to determine who can do the most for mankind.

Mr. Khrushchev also knows, as we do, that a competition is not likely to remain peaceful unless both sides understand the rules and are willing to have them fairly enforced by an impartial umpire. He has pointedly reminded the world that Soviet troops are not in Germany to play skittles. The free nations passionately wish that Mr. Khrushchev's troops, as well as their own, could find it possible to play more skittles and less atomic war games. But we remind him that his troops could not even play skittles without rules of the game.

If the Soviets really mean this talk of peaceful competition, then they have nothing to fear from impartial rules impartially judged which will make such peaceful competition possible.

The Soviet leaders claim to be acutely aware of the lessons of history. They are constantly quoting the past to prove their contention that communism is the wave of the future. May I call to their attention one striking conclusion that is found in every page of recorded history. It is this: the advance of civilization, the growth of culture, and the perfection of all the finest qualities of mankind have all been accomplished by respect for law and justice and by the constant growth of the use of law in place of force.

The barbarian, the outlaw, the bandit are symbols of a civilization that is either primitive or decadent. As men grow in wisdom, they recognize that might does not make right;

that true liberty is freedom under law; and that the arrogance of power is a pitiful substitute for justice and equity.

Hence once again we say to those in the Kremlin who boast of the superiority of their system: Let us compete in peace, and let our course of action be such that the choice we offer uncommitted nations is not a choice between progress and reaction, between high civilization and a return to barbarism, between the rule of law and the rule of force.

In a context of justice, of concern for the millions of men and women who yearn for peace, of a constant striving to bring the wealth abounding in this earth to those who today languish in hunger and want—in such a context, competition between the Communist world and the free world would indeed be meaningful. Then we could say without hesitation: let the stronger system win, knowing that both systems would be moving in the direction of a world at peace, with increasing material prosperity serving as a foundation for a flowering of the human spirit.

We could then put aside the hatred and distrust of the past and work for a better world. Our goal will be peace. Our instrument for achieving peace will be law and justice. Our hope will be that, under these conditions, the vast energies now devoted to weapons of war will instead be used to clothe, house, and feed the entire world. This is the only goal worthy of our aspirations. Competing in this way, nobody will lose, and mankind will gain.

2. *Foreign Aid* [8]

No nation in history has spent more of its material wealth and manpower in the interests of the community of free nations than the United States has in the past fifty years. From 1945 to 1958 we spent 64 billion dollars for foreign economic and military aid and 382.2 billion dollars for military preparedness at home. Fifty-three thousand four hundred Americans died in World War I. Two-hundred-ninety-one thousand five hundred died in World War II. Thirty-three thousand six hundred died in Korea. Two million six hundred thousand Americans are under arms today.

Why this huge expenditure of money and manpower?

[8] The material in this section is derived from the following sources:

Remarks at Conference on India and the United States, Washington, D.C. May 4, 1959. Responses to questions at the California Newspaper Publishers Association Convention, Los Angeles, California. February 6, 1960. Remarks at the Fourth Annual Luncheon of the General Conference of CBS Television Affiliates, Washington, D.C. January 13, 1958. Remarks at the National Brotherhood Award Dinner of the National Conference of Christians and Jews, Cleveland, Ohio. February 27, 1958. Address to The Pilgrims, London, England. November 25, 1958. Address to the Sixty-sixth Annual Convention of the General Federation of Women's Clubs, Asheville, North Carolina. June 5, 1957. Remarks to the U.S. Junior Chamber of Commerce Convention, Milwaukee, Wisconsin. June 25, 1957. Remarks to the Forty-second Annual Kiwanis International Convention, Atlantic City, New Jersey. June 27, 1957. Responses to questions at the Conference with Representatives of the Four Armed Services, Washington, D.C. July 29, 1957. Remarks to the International Industrial Development Conference, San Francisco, California. October 15, 1957. "The Greater Menace," Address at the Conference on University Contracts Abroad sponsored by the Committee on Institutional Projects Abroad of the American Council on Education, Denver, Colorado. November 14–15, 1957. Remarks at the National Defense Executive Reserve Conference, Washington, D.C. November 13, 1957. Remarks at the Annual Meeting of the National Association of Manufacturers, New York, New York. December 6, 1957.

Not because we want territory; we have asked for none and we have acquired none.

Not because we want the countries we aid to be dependent upon us; but because we want them to be strong enough to be independent of any foreign domination.

Not because we want war; but because we want peace.

We have heard a great deal of criticism over the years of our foreign-aid programs. There are some who would have us believe that these programs amount to nothing more than a great philanthropic giveaway to undeserving and unappreciative foreigners. If this were indeed the case, the Congress would not be justified in appropriating a dollar for their continuance.

Let us examine our aid programs solely in terms of one question: are they serving the interests of the United States?

Approximately three-fourths of a typical annual foreign-aid appropriation is for military assistance. Among the countries which are receiving military assistance are: South Korea, Formosa, South Viet Nam, Pakistan, and Turkey. All of these countries have common borders with Communist nations. We know from what happened in Korea that if these countries are not strong enough to defend themselves they run the risk of attack. If they are attacked, we would inevitably become involved.

The question then is not whether they should have adequate defense forces, but how it can be done most economically and effectively.

On the average it costs five times as much to maintain an American soldier abroad as it does to maintain a fighting man of the allies we are aiding. By conservative estimates, an expenditure of $2.8 billion in United States foreign military aid results directly in at least $15 billion worth of defense for ourselves and the free world. Spending less for military aid abroad would simply mean spending more for defense at home —and more American boys in uniform.

I submit that on the basis of these facts those who would substantially cut or eliminate our military foreign-aid programs are in fact the spendthrifts and not the economizers.

Might I emphasize that we cannot be too concerned about maintaining our alliances and allocating the funds necessary to support them when we know that it is through this strength that we have peace in the world today. All of us will agree that it is far better to maintain our armed forces in peace than to have to send our young men abroad in time of war.

As an illustration of just how effective military alliances among free nations can be, let us look for a moment at NATO. The group of nations with which we are associated in NATO have a combined economic and military strength which, added to ours, assures security against attack. The alliance has been truly historic. And it has not coveted a foot of foreign soil. It has not interfered in the internal problems of member nations. Its sole concern has been defense against aggression and the safeguarding of freedom. The question is often raised: just exactly how solid is this alliance?

It is true we had difficulties during the Suez crisis with two of our oldest and firmest allies, France and Britain. But that crisis has now receded into the background. We are finding, and have found, that the things that draw us together—as much a common cultural heritage as a present military threat— are infinitely stronger than the things that would drive us apart. I am convinced that today our NATO alliance is stronger, militarily, economically, and politically than it has been at any time since World War II.

Of course NATO is not without problems. It is, after all, an alliance of free nations. No nation has been compelled to join. None would be forbidden to leave. Individual member nations may have differences with other member nations. Some see the need for readjustment of responsibilities within the alliance. These matters are discussed with mature wisdom and prudent restraint. But regardless of the solutions proposed or achieved, the transcendent need for unity in the face of continuing threats to world peace requires that no issue should be allowed to divide us.

We have to realize that our present position of world responsibility is a new one for the people of the United States. Our country has developed very, very fast during the 350 years since the first colonists landed at Jamestown. Our experience in the field of foreign policy is comparatively limited, and we are very impatient every time anything goes wrong. We would like every policy, every action that we take in the world, to be immediately crowned with success. What we have to realize is that we must grow up. We must be mature in our reactions to events around the world. We must assume that some of the things we do will not be successful, that mistakes will be made.

What we must always do is to weigh the long-range gains against the short-range defeats that we may suffer. And if, on balance, we are going steadily forward, then we must continue to support our policies.

In this connection, let us remember that the stationing of American troops in foreign countries in times of peace is also a new development. In wartime this is understood; it is difficult even then, but it is tolerated. But in times of peace it is infinitely more difficult. Even though there are alliances between the United States and those countries in which our men are stationed, this arrangement is very hard to maintain, and a few incidents are almost inevitable.

As we look at our alliances around the world, therefore, we should never allow little irritations that may develop in this country or that one between our allies and ourselves to make us feel that we should get rid of our world responsibilities.

I do not doubt that the United States will continue to

appropriate the funds necessary for sustaining our military alliances and military-aid programs. Having recognized these fundamental facts, however, let me turn to a less encouraging field.

I submit that the greatest danger which confronts the United States and the free world is not that we will be in a position of military weakness against the Soviet Union or the Communist empire. I do not think that time will come, because I think we are capable of meeting that threat. But the greatest danger is in failing to recognize the threat which is presented to us in these other fields where history tells us the Communists have been more effective in accomplishing their objectives —the fields of economic, political, and psychological warfare.

Just how great is this threat? In 1957 the Soviet Union celebrated the fortieth year of the coming to power of the Communist government in Russia. It is hard to realize that just forty years before, there were only 80,000 Communist Party members in Russia. What had they been able to do by 1957? During that forty years the number of people in the world under the control of Communist governments went from 80,000 to 1 billion. How did it happen?

The empires of the past generally grew through military aggression, but this Communist empire has grown in an altogether different way. In no substantial instance has the Communist empire gained new territory or new people by traditional overt aggression across a border. They came to power in Russia through revolution. They came to power in Communist China in the same way. They came to power in the satellite countries through *coups d'état,* again through means other than overt aggression.

I would not want to suggest that military power has had no relationship to the Communists' success. By reason of their considerable military power and the pressure they can exert with it, they have been able to blackmail other countries into submission. In countries that they presently control, such as Hungary, they have used military force to put down whatever revolutions might occur.

Nevertheless, as we examine the record, there is no question but that the major danger the free world faces today is not overt aggression. The major danger, the surest danger, the war that has been, is being, and will continue to be waged against us is in the political, the economic, the psychological, and the subversive fields.

Having said this, let us examine the present battlefield and see what the stages are. It is often said that the world is divided into thirds these days. Approximately a billion of the world's people are under Communist domination; a billion are in the free world, allied with us and other free nations; and the remaining billion, most of them inhabitants of Asia, Africa, and the Near East, constitute the so-called "uncommitted" third. The battleground in which the Soviet Union is now pinpointing its economic and political and psychological warfare is this uncommitted world. Why? First, because they know that this area is much easier to penetrate than the allied countries, the more developed countries; and, second, because they realize that if they can win a major part of the uncommitted world to the Communist side, they will have the economic and the human resources to dominate the rest of the world—in effect, to force the free world into a subordinate position and perhaps into eventual economic or political surrender.

How grave is the danger? Let us see what the Communists are doing in this field. During the first ten years after World War II, the United States spent approximately $60 billion in foreign aid. This includes the Marshall Plan, of course. It includes economic assistance to the newly developing countries in Asia, Africa, and the Near East. It includes military aid as well. The Soviet Union during that same period expended approximately one-tenth as much—$6 billion. Why, then, do they pose any problem for us? Because they are able to concentrate their economic assistance in the areas of greatest weakness.

They move in where they think the government is unstable. They move in where a government needs funds to maintain economic progress and is unable to get them elsewhere. When they do move in, they do so with one thought in mind and one only: that by assisting the country, they will gain the power eventually to dominate it.

As we look to the future we must realize that if we leave a vacuum in these uncommitted areas of the world it is not going to remain unfilled. I do not mean that the Soviet Union is going to aid every one of the countries that does not get aid from the United States or other free nations. But I do mean that in any particular area or country where the Communists see that through aid they may be able to achieve power, they will move in.

When the Communists help countries abroad, you can be sure that they do not do it for any philanthropic reasons. They do it at a time when their own standard of living is low, when their own people are desperately poor. They provide economic assistance to countries abroad for the single reason that it serves them in their plans for world conquest. And at the present time, the Soviet Union is stepping up the amount of economic assistance it is offering, particularly to this uncommitted world.

On an average, the United States is now spending a billion dollars a year to provide economic assistance to nations abroad. Most of this money goes to countries in Africa, the Near East, and Asia—and, increasingly, to Latin America, too.

I have visited most of the countries involved. I have seen our economic assistance programs in operation. There has been some waste and inefficiency in their administration. But when we consider the tremendous stakes involved, we can only conclude that the remedy for these difficulties and errors is to try to do a more effective job, not to give up and let the Soviet Union start taking over the world by default.

You often hear it said, "You can't buy friends." I agree completely. The purpose of our aid is not to buy the friendship of these countries and not to make them satellites. We aid them in order to toughen their economic and political fiber to a point where they can be independent of any foreign domination—including our own.

There is one fundamental principle we must always have in mind in the world conflict: the most deadly enemy to the Communist objective of world domination is independence. That is the one thing they cannot tolerate. Take, for example, the case of Tito's Yugoslavia. It certainly cannot be said that Tito is allied with the free world. I would say that Tito is simply allied with Tito. His actions in the past few years, when he first broke with Stalin and since that time, have all been dictated by self-interest. Although we could hardly base our policy on the assumption that in the event of a conflict Tito will be with us, we must nevertheless encourage him in the independent stand he is taking. It is far better for Tito to be neutral—even if his kind of neutrality benefits us little—than it is for him to be simply another satellite completely under the control of the Soviet Union. That is why Titoism is such anathema to all the top Communists in the Soviet Union.

How then can we justify the allocation of government funds when we agree at the outset that these funds may not, in some instances, obtain complete agreement with the policies of the United States? My answer is this: our stake, the free world's stake, in these newly developing countries is that they should achieve the economic stability which will enable them in turn to maintain political independence.

As a further case in point, you will hear people say that because President Sukarno has indicated some approval of the kind of government activities he saw in Communist China, Indonesia should be written off. You will hear people say that the United States should under no circumstances continue to provide economic assistance to Indonesia—that Indonesia is too far gone to receive any more consideration because of its leadership.

Let us examine Mr. Sukarno for a moment. First, he is a leader of great magnetism, one of the finest orators in the world, perhaps the best when it comes to holding a great crowd. Second, he is a man who admires some of America's historical leaders. When he was here, and when I visited him four years ago, he expressed particular admiration for George Washington and for Abraham Lincoln. He said: "After all, when I was in school they were my heroes." Third, there is no doubt in my mind at all but that Sukarno would prefer to have an Indonesia which was not dominated by a Communist-type government. He may not see the Communist threat as we see it, but I do not think we can question, in the long run, his devotion to basic ideals of freedom.

If this is true, why is he doing what he is doing? Part of this goes back to the legacy with which colonialism endowed Indonesia. Indonesia is a rich country agriculturally—so rich that a peasant can grow from a plot the size of a tennis court enough to feed a family of six or eight people. It is a country which, after it won its independence from the Dutch, found that it had been torn to pieces by the struggle which was necessary to achieve that independence. And after it won its independence, what Indonesia lacked above everything else was leadership. Under the colonial policy which had dominated that country through the years, no trained leaders in government and business, so badly needed to run such a populous country stretching over thousands of miles of islands, had been developed.

This is Sukarno's problem. How can he run such a country as a Western-style democracy? He is convinced at the moment, apparently, that he cannot apply the same principles that have been effective here. I do not think, however, that we should assume that because he feels a different approach to Indonesian problems is necessary, he and his people should be written off and allowed to fall under Communist domination.

Too much of value is involved. Indonesia has 90 million people. It is the gateway to all of the Pacific, to Australia, to New Zealand, and then, of course, to the sea which touches upon Ceylon and India. Indonesia, Malaya, Ceylon, and all of the countries in that complex are in the Asian trading area which is absolutely vital to the economic survival of Japan. If Japan does not trade with China, it must develop substitute trading areas in Southeast Asia.

Indonesia, coming under Communist domination, might set in motion a chain reaction which would orient the whole of Southeast Asia toward communism. Such a development could be disastrous as far as Asia is concerned, if only for the effect it would have on Japan.

We simply cannot approach these international problems country by country. We have to approach them with a keen sense of history and geography. That is one thing that our potential enemies in the Kremlin and in Peiping have always done. Each country, with its problems, is related to all the others.

There is in Asia today the basis for a fascinating—and deadly —comparison. There are two great peoples in Asia: those who live under the Communist government of China, and the people of India. These are the two greatest population centers not only of Asia but of the world. One is attempting to achieve economic progress by forced draft, under conditions of slavery. The other is attempting to achieve economic progress with freedom. These two nations are very different in many respects, but they are alike in this one—they both need and they both want economic progress.

The question which will be answered in the next decades will be this: can a people who need economic progress to satisfy the wants of their greatly increasing population achieve it in a climate of freedom, or must they pay for progress by giving up their freedom? What happens in India will have a tremendous impact on the decisions made in other countries in Asia, in the Near East, in Africa, and even in the Americas. Here we have an indication of the tremendous stake of the free world in the economic problems of India and other countries like India.

It is for this reason that I maintain that our program of loans and technical aid to such countries is just as essential to our survival as the production of missiles and aircraft.

But too often we consider the importance of a country like India merely in relation to the security of the free world. This is not our sole interest, either as a government or as a people, when we provide governmental or other assistance to our friends in India. If there were no communism in the world, if there were no other similar threat to our freedom, there would still be poverty and misery and disease. And the people of the United States and our government would still be concerned about helping to wipe out that poverty and misery and disease.

I would not like the case for United States assistance to rest simply on the negative, defensive issue of helping the have-not nations in order to save the United States from communism. I think the case can be more accurately and more forcefully presented not in terms of the defeat of communism but rather of the victory of plenty over want, of health over disease, of freedom over tyranny of any type, wherever it exists in the world. We can assure our friends in these lands that we welcome the opportunity to work with them in developing the economic progress which they desire, so that they can prove to all the world that it is possible to have progress with freedom. This is our aim, and we know also that it is theirs.

I am confident that we can meet the economic challenge provided we base our aid policies on the fundamental principle which is the generating force behind our whole way of life—the recognition that the most productive source of economic progress is private rather than government enterprise.

Private initiative, private responsibility, and private capital are the motors of economic progress. The economic growth which can thus be generated is vital to the future of the whole free world.

I say this fully recognizing that there has been and is an important place for government action, and that government capital will have a vital role to play as long as the world crisis is with us. Wherever it has an opportunity to strengthen free economies against the shoddy temptations of Communist trade or the menace of Communist subversion, I believe we should use this weapon of government finance as boldly as Congress will permit.

However, we must recognize that government capital is, in a sense, crisis capital. It cannot possibly meet the long-run problem with which we are confronted. The total amount of investment which must flow from capital-surplus areas like the United States to capital-deficit areas during the next few years must substantially increase rather than decrease. The only source of investment funds that can be greatly expanded is private capital. It is, consequently, the only source that can possibly meet the need.

There is a limit to what government can do. There is partly the limit imposed by budgetary problems. But above all there is the limit imposed by our positive conviction that free private enterprise is the preferable medium for aid for the newly developing countries.

In many nations the pattern of economic development is being shaped for a century ahead. If this pattern is statist, then human freedom will be the loser.

Freedom is essentially personal. It is exercised only with great difficulty through impersonal groups. For this reason it is vital that newly developing economic systems, so far as possible, follow a pattern that fosters rather than limits human freedom.

Private capital has other merits which government capital lacks. It is the kind of money which, in the old Roman phrase, has no smell. Its home government cannot order it to be spent in one country rather than another, and cannot attach political or diplomatic strings to its use.

It carries no ideology with it, other than the reasonable expectation of safety and profit. But it does carry something else with it: brains. The managerial skills and imagination behind private capital are the best assurance that it will in fact create the new wealth that both lender and borrower are aiming at.

We need, then, a spectacular increase of investment by American and other free world businessmen, directed especially to the newly developing nations of the world.

What should be the goal of private United States capital in this field? In 1958 new American investment abroad totaled almost $4 billion. This amount seems large, but if the United States were investing abroad the same proportion of its national income that Great Britain invested abroad in 1910, we would be investing not $4 billion a year but nearly $30 billion!

I do not suggest that we could recapture the world of 1910 even if we wanted to. But certainly it is not unreasonable to set as our goal doubling or tripling private American investment abroad in the next ten years. But we cannot expect this to happen automatically.

There are certain things which the United States government can do, that the governments of countries in which money is to be invested can do, and that American businessmen abroad can do, to stimulate the increase in foreign investment the world needs.

First, let us consider what steps the capital-deficit nations can take to encourage private investment from abroad. There must be, at the outset, recognition of the fact that the world shortage of capital which evidences itself in rising interest rates has forced a sharp measure of competition for the limited capital which is available for foreign investment. Any government that is serious about wanting private capital will necessarily enter this competition. It can set such conditions as will either induce that capital to flow or stop it cold. It can treat foreign capital as something between a public enemy and a necessary evil, or it can make the kind of rules under which private capital can do its best work.

Let me give an example. Whatever one may think of Premier Nasser's right to "Egyptianize" the Suez Canal—and our government has not disputed his right—it cannot be denied that he made Egypt less attractive to new capital than it was before. In contrast we see the results in countries like the Netherlands, Northern Ireland, Mexico, or our own independent Commonwealth of Puerto Rico, where the governments have set up active and efficient bureaus and hospitable policies to promote and welcome foreign capital. And as a result, they are getting more of it than ever before.

The government of the United States would never presume to tell any other government what its policy should be toward foreign investment, but the owners of private capital will inevitably take note of the investment climate before moving abroad.

Let us now see what the government of the United States can and should do to encourage private investment abroad. I would suggest the following as a minimum program for consideration:

The economic sections of our embassies abroad should be upgraded and strengthened both in quantity and quality. Every American embassy should be staffed with qualified personnel who can devote an adequate amount of their time and energy to the active promotion of policies which encourage private investment.

When tax revision becomes feasible, the Congress should pass a tax reform which would extend to American investors in other parts of the world the fourteen-point income tax credit for which Western Hemisphere trade corporations are already eligible.

The Congress should also consider the feasibility of passing a tax reform similar to one adopted by the United Kingdom two years ago. This would defer United States taxes on income and profits earned entirely abroad until they are actually paid in dividends to stockholders of the parent company. It would immediately increase the funds available to such companies for additional foreign investment. Yet in the long run the United States Treasury would gain by the tax on income from a larger investment base.

We should channel more of our governmental financial operations abroad through private investors and enterprisers, United States and foreign. Specifically, Congress could require (instead of permitting as at present) that at least 25 per cent of the foreign currencies we now acquire under our agricultural-aid program be made available for loans to American firms in those countries.

The new $300 million developmental fund should be operated in such a way that in its administration and policies it does not become merely a pale carbon copy of either the Export-Import Bank or the ICA. The Administration and the Congress intended that this fund fill a function which is new and distinct from those being served by existing agencies. Its primary purpose should be to channel funds into private enterprises which cannot satisfy the borrowing requirements of the Export-Import Bank.

We should intensify, through international organizations such as the World Bank, studies to examine the feasibility of setting up a privately operated international investment guarantee fund. Its object would be to protect both present and future investments from the hazards of expropriation, devaluation, blocked currencies, and similar risks.

Trade is, perhaps more than any other factor, the great generator and vehicle of the capital the world so badly needs. Our trade policies have a great impact on other nations, and particularly on our allies. Let us take, as an example, Japan. We have been trying to encourage Japan not to develop too close relations with Communist China, for obvious reasons.

If Japan should ever go behind the Iron Curtain, the tremendous industrial force of the Japanese people would be on the side of the slave nations, and that could be decisive not only in the Pacific, but all over the world.

Japan's major problem is simply to exist. The Japanese are a very productive people, but they have in Japan, I think, only about one-tenth as much tillable land as they have in the State of California. It is remarkable that nearly 90 million people are able to maintain the economy that they do under such circumstances.

Clearly, the Japanese must trade with somebody. If they do not trade with Communist China, where are they going to go? They can trade with Southeast Asia, and they can trade with the United States.

The moment that we erect tariff barriers which have the effect of keeping Japanese products out, we force the Japanese into another area of trade which might mean developments harmful to our basic interest.

I could give other examples, but certainly this is one of the best to indicate that when we develop a trade policy in the United States, it has a tremendous effect abroad. And we must always develop our policies having in mind not only the interests of our own farmers, our own manufacturers, our own workers—as we should—but also the broad interest of American foreign policy.

The Reciprocal Trade Agreements Act should be extended

for at least five years when it next comes up for Congressional renewal. This action would demonstrate permanent and expanding United States interest in world trade. Whether in order to get paid for our exports, or to get a return on our investments, or simply to assure ourselves of the most economical source of raw materials, the United States must become an ever larger importer. The Reciprocal Trade Agreements Act is our best assurance that imports will be accessible to us on a fair and nondiscriminatory basis.

For the same reason we should complete our membership in the Organization for Trade Cooperation. This organization, which the United States helped to found, is a clearing house where the established system of multilateral tariff bargaining and the rules of trade reciprocity can be recorded and systematized. It asks nothing of us that we have not already been doing. Not to join it officially would be an act of gross self-deception and would mislead the rest of the world as to our real interest and policy.

We should pass legislation, long since recommended by the President, to simplify certain antiquated and unjust methods of valuation in our customs procedures. In the long run, it must be the policy of the United States to lower the barriers which presently restrict trade between countries, because we believe that for nations to trade with each other is one of the most salutary ways to reduce potential international tensions.

So much, in brief, for what our government can do. There are also certain obligations that businessmen should assume if they are to share in the increased opportunities for trade and investment abroad.

Their investment operations must be based, first of all, on the twentieth-century principle that the primary purpose of foreign investment is to create new wealth rather than to exploit a newly developing country.

American personnel abroad should always be trained to be ambassadors of good will as well as competent technicians.

The training of foreign nationals to assume managerial as well as subordinate responsibilities should be given top priority.

I would not suggest that these proposals I have recommended are all-inclusive, but the adoption of such a program could provide the necessary stimulus for a dramatic expansion of private investment and trade throughout the world.

We should never make the mistake of assuming that the problems involved in winning the friendship and allegiance of the peoples of the uncommitted nations are entirely economic, or that purely economic policies will solve them.

The people of these countries above all else want and deserve recognition of their dignity as individuals and as nations. In my opinion the major reason for the opposition to colonialism in Asia and Africa was not economic exploitation or even the denial of independence, but the age-old resentments engendered by the notion of white superiority.

We must avoid any American action that seems to imply that we feel we are a superior breed. If we cannot treat the newly independent nations of Asia and Africa, or for that matter any sovereign people, as our moral equals, we had better abandon our struggle against communism and be prepared for ultimate conquest. The greatest sin we can be guilty of in the international field is that of arrogance, of false pride, and failure to recognize and respect human dignity.

I can testify from personal experience on this score on the basis of visits to over fifty countries in the past eight years. In my opinion, there is a great well of friendship for the people of the United States among the people of other lands. All we have to do is to go halfway in treating them as equals, in respecting their traditions, and in proceeding always on the basic assumption that there are no second-class nations in the world today. Nothing can contribute more to the cause of peace than for us to act and think in those terms in our dealings with other peoples.

Then there is the matter of simple public relations. This directly involves our overseas information service. A modern concept of sound industrial public relations is to inform the people properly of the activities of a company. It is just as simple and equally as sound a concept that the United States, which does much that is good, should tell its story to the peoples of the world. This is particularly important when our competitors, the Communists, are spending each year an estimated five times as much as we are in the propaganda and information field.

You have no doubt read some of the caustic criticisms of our information program. I would not for one instant contend that everything we have done in this field has produced good results. But public relations for a business is at best an inexact science. In the case of government, where the problem is selling ideas rather than goods, the problem is infinitely more difficult.

We must not allow our failures in this field to blind us to the fundamental truth that it is penny-wise and pound-foolish to spend billions to create a good product and then not spend the few millions necessary to sell it.

We can have real peace in the world only when we have understanding among people as well as among diplomats. That is why another of our most potent weapons for peace is the program of person-to-person contacts among citizens of various nations.

Our government brings each year about 8,000 leaders from other nations to study our country and its people. These people are specialists in such fields as politics, social welfare, labor, agriculture, health, the press, and education. The impression they receive of America will have a tremendous effect in determining the climate of world opinion about our democratic system.

We do not wish to organize propaganda tours for these visitors such as the Russians do for carefully guided teams of tourists and other representatives of the free world. We want them to see our democracy in action as it really is.

I am confident that when such visitors are invited to typical American homes they will be given a lasting impression of the essential decency of our people.

These are simple things, all of them, and yet they need constant remembering.

The world of tomorrow is in our hands.

It can be a world of peace, with political freedom, economic growth, and the steady abolition of poverty.

But it can also be a world of hatred and suspicion, perpetually on the verge of war.

It can be a free world, or it can be poisoned by statism or totalitarianism.

It can produce for the needs of families, or it can produce for the needs of armies.

The choice between these two worlds must be made by our own generation. If freedom loses, it may be a century before it can be regained. We ourselves may be starved for essential new materials and crushed without a single warlike act.

Americans can never again live in isolation. Either we march into the future, together with other free nations, into a world of peace and prosperity, or we decline into obscurity and failure, as a people who had not the vision to see the world as it is or who had not the courage to face up to its clear duty.

3.   The Pursuit of Peace [9]

One of the first questions that often arises in any discussion of international affairs goes something like this: what can the United Nations do to work toward the peaceful settlement of international differences?

There are a number of ways in which the United Nations can contribute to better understanding in the world and to world peace, and I would list in particular these three areas:

First, the United Nations has already proved that it can be very useful in settling minor disputes between nations, disputes which in years past might have resulted in armed conflict.

Second, the United Nations is doing work in some fields that very few people know about but in which it is making a long-range contribution to better understanding, not only among free nations and neutral nations, but even between the free world and the Communist world. A good example of the kind of work I am referring to is the activity of the World Health Organization, in which people from all over the world work together for a cause about which there can be no disagreement. This kind of project can only be helpful to the cause of peace.

[9] The material in this section is derived from the following sources:
Responses to questions at the California Newspaper Publishers Association Convention, Los Angeles, California. February 6, 1960. Responses to questions at the Economic Club of Detroit, Detroit, Michigan. February 15, 1960. Remarks at the National Brotherhood Award Dinner of the National Conference of Christians and Jews, Cleveland, Ohio. February 27, 1958. Remarks at the All-Congress Dinner of the 1958 National Nuclear Energy Congress, Chicago, Illinois. March 19, 1958. Remarks at the Sixty-sixth Annual Convention of the General Federation of Women's Clubs, Asheville, North Carolina. June 5, 1957. Remarks at the U.S. Junior Chamber of Commerce Convention, Milwaukee, Wisconsin. June 25, 1957. Responses to questions at the Conference with Representatives of the Four Armed Services, Washington, D.C. July 29, 1957.

Third, the United Nations provides a forum in which the great nations of the world along with the small ones can meet across the conference table. Through that forum the force of world public opinion can be brought to bear whenever any nation gets out of line.

Now I do not mean by this that world public opinion developed through the United Nations can, all by itself, control the action of an aggressor nation or a violating nation. As the situation in Hungary proved, this is not always possible.

On the other hand, using the same example, the United Nations report on Hungary certainly cost the Soviet Union a great deal of its prestige and effectiveness in the neutral world and even among the satellites, because the United Nations report gave the lie to the propaganda dispensed by both the Soviet Union and its puppet regime in Hungary to the effect that this was not a popular revolt but was inspired and supported from outside.

Obviously, however, under present world conditions there are limits to the work that an organization like the United Nations can do. Certain issues must be tackled by the great powers that alone are involved. Diplomacy at all levels must be brought to bear on these issues. There are times when it is appropriate, and even essential, to resort to summit talks.

There is considerable confusion about the American attitude toward summit talks. This is true not only in the United States, but also among our allies and friends abroad.

The favorite cliché of those who advocate summit talks regardless of the circumstances is, "Talking is always better than fighting." This, however, is not the only choice. Talking is not better than not talking when you do not know what you are going to talk about.

Our responsible diplomats are more than willing to negotiate with the Soviet leaders. But summit talks must—and can—

follow only after the paths of normal diplomacy have been traced to their logical conclusion.

In any event, no one summit conference is going to solve the very grave differences that exist between the United States and the free world, on the one hand, and the Communist bloc, on the other.

Summit talks can provide an opportunity to discuss some of the current problems most at issue between us to make at least some progress toward their solution. But we do not on our side, and the Soviet Union should not on its side, expect that any one conference is going to solve these problems. Our differences are so deep that it is going to take a period of years to reduce those areas of disagreement which exist between us.

We must not, however, adopt a negative position in regard to negotiations with the Soviets. In this country, people often ask: "What is to be gained by trying to negotiate specific problems with the Russians, since the past record indicates that Communist promises aren't worth the paper they're written on?" I agree with this general appraisal as to what Communist agreements are worth. History has shown us that time after time they make a solemn agreement and then break it if it suits their purposes.

But what is our alternative to these conferences and negotiations? The alternative—to have no negotiations—would mean, obviously, that we would lessen our chances of achieving agreements with the Communists—slim as these chances might be. And that might mean, in turn, heading into an armed clash which could destroy civilization as we know it.

Then too, as we know, there is a great battle going on in the world, not only militarily and economically, but also ideologically. The greater part of the world which has yet to make up its mind which way to turn would not understand if the free world rejected any attempts to negotiate our differences when the Communist world appears willing to do so. So, to the world we must clearly and unequivocally delineate our attitude and our determination:

That we have and will negotiate with the Soviet leaders.

That wherever there has been reasonable opportunity to reach agreement, the United States has sought it out and will continue to do so.

A third reason for continuing to encourage these summit conferences is that although, generally speaking, the Communists do not agree to anything unless they think it is going to serve their purposes and often break the agreements they do make, in some instances they have made agreements that have helped the cause of freedom and peace.

Let's take for example the Austrian Peace Treaty. This took a long time to negotiate. At times people were about ready to give up. But eventually a settlement was reached. And now we find Austria developing as a strong independent country. This would not have happened unless we had persisted in our attempts to work out an agreement with the Communists.

In dealing with the Communists we have to be very sure that we do not make agreements on the basis of faith alone. We must be positive that the agreements are to the greatest possible extent self-enforcing.

One sensible approach is to try to formulate agreements in which the Soviet Union's self-interest will require that it live up to the obligation. This approach points to a long, hard road ahead of us. In many areas Soviet self-interest is such that the only kind of agreement that could be reached would be one which would weaken the position of the free world and strengthen the position of the Soviet world. But this does not mean that we should not continue to try.

I think it can be safely said that there are *some* areas of give-and-take wherever there are differences between nations at the conference table. But we must distinguish between flexibility with regard to tactics and flexibility with regard to principle. I know that Mr. Dulles, for example, was often criticized as being inflexible. I would say that his inflexibility was a position that he took in firm adherence to and advocacy of the basic principles of freedom and justice, principles which we in the United States share with people throughout the free world and which we simply cannot compromise. This kind of inflexibility is what the United States should continue to want from its foreign-policy leaders.

Here is a case in point. Mr. Khrushchev, when I talked with him in Moscow, spoke of the trade restrictions between our two countries, which he wanted to see relaxed.

As long as tensions exist in the world, as a result of aggressive Soviet policies which brought about trade restrictions, those restrictions *insofar as strategic goods are concerned* will have to remain. Only when the U.S.S.R. changes the policies which have created these tensions, only when we can be convinced that they will not use their power aggressively against us, can the restrictions on trade in strategic goods be lifted.

In point of fact, we should be under no illusions about how much trade would be increased between the Soviet Union and the United States even with a lifting of restrictions. The question is not whether the Soviet Union wants to buy things from us, but whether they have anything to sell to us in return.

Let us consider one item, manganese. We used to buy manganese from the Soviet Union, but shortly after the war they cut off our market. We went to India and to Turkey to develop new sources for manganese. Now at the present time the Soviet Union would like to sell manganese to us so that they could buy things in return. After they took the initiative in denying us this product, do we now turn to the Indians and the Turks and say: "You built these mines up, partly in answer to our demand, but we're not going to buy from you any more, since the Soviet Union is going to let us buy from them again"? Of course not.

That is exactly what I said to Mr. Khrushchev when we discussed future United States–Soviet trade.

Shortly before my trip to the Soviet Union I was talking to an expert on Soviet affairs, who formerly was with the State Department. This question of the reliability of the Communists arose. A third party to the conversation put it this way: Is Mr. Khrushchev sincere when he says he is for disarmament? Is he sincere when he says he is for peace and for peaceful competition, ruling out the use of force as a means of realizing the Communist objective of world domination?

This was the Soviet expert's answer: You should not even use the word "sincere" in connection with Mr. Khrushchev or any other Communist, because Communist standards with regard to motives are different from ours. The Communist is a materialist. We in the West are basically idealistic. "Sincere" is a word that describes an idealist. It is one that cannot describe the materialist.

And then he used this analogy: You can no more describe a Communist motive as being sincere than you can describe a table or chair as being sincere, because it is impossible for the Communist to think in Western idealistic terms.

Now this does not mean, he said, that Mr. Khrushchev may not be for disarmament at one particular time or another. It does not mean that Mr. Khrushchev and the Communist leaders are not for peace. It does not mean that they are against an accommodation with the Western powers on the Berlin situation, for instance.

It only means that in determining whether they want these things we should not say: "Well, they are sincere because they love peace as an end in itself, or disarmament as an end in itself." We should not assume that the relationship between their actions and their motives is the same as ours.

What we must do is ask what their objective is. Their objective was, is now, and will continue to be a Communist-dominated world. Therefore anything they stand for in the field of foreign policy must be designed to further that objective. At any given time, for example, being for disarmament may better serve that objective than being against it—because of their desire to gain support among the uncommitted peoples of the world, and also because they need more consumer goods for the hard-pressed Russian workers.

The point is simply that it is very dangerous and unrealistic to attempt to judge the Communists by our standards. We have to bear in mind constantly that the Communist is a materialist, a realist, and a fanatically dedicated individual determined to do anything and everything he can that will serve his precise purposes.

If we judge every Communist move and motive in these terms, we will be close to a true analysis of what he really wants or thinks at any particular moment.

The unqualified dedication of the government and people of the United States to the cause of peace cannot seriously be questioned by anyone who knows our record in international affairs. But some of our friends, as well as our opponents, have questioned whether our policies are designed to further that objective. Let us examine some of the criticisms that have been made.

Why do we not accept the Soviet proposal for stopping atomic tests? [10]

We can have honest disagreement over such issues as the extent of the danger from nuclear fall-out if tests are not con-

---

[10] This material is drawn from 1958 sources and refers to Soviet proposals current at that time. But in 1960, at the two simultaneous Geneva conferences on disarmament and on nuclear testing, the Soviet Union presented substantially the same proposals: immediate suspension of all open tests of nuclear weapons, a moratorium on undetectable underground tests, and rapid "complete and total" disarmament, without, however, going into any detail about inspection and control systems. It has been the consistent U.S. position, on the other hand, that foolproof control is absolutely central to any agreements in these fields.

trolled, the possibility that secret underground tests may be able to evade any inspection system, and whether testing is necessary for full development of the peaceful uses of atomic energy.

But let us have no illusions on the major issue.

Stopping tests is not in itself going to reduce the danger of war. The types of weapons already in production are adequate to carry out their mission of massive destruction. That is why control of *production* as well as tests of nuclear weapons, as the United States has proposed, is the only formula which goes to the heart of the problem.

The same considerations are involved in the United States position on general disarmament.

There is no question as to our desire to enter into a disarmament agreement. The problem is in securing an agreement that is enforcible—because an agreement without adequate inspection provisions, which one party might honor and the other might not, would seriously and perhaps fatally increase rather than reduce the risk of war.

I know there are those who suggest that we can make reductions in our defense establishment because of the prospects for disarmament. But the period in which negotiations for disarmament are taking place is the very time when we must not reduce our defenses.

Our primary objective in such negotiations must not be to reduce a burden of armaments we are unable or unwilling to maintain, but to reduce the danger of war which our armed strength is designed to prevent.

The road to war is paved with agreements based solely on mutual trust. That is why we best serve the cause of peace when we insist that any disarmament agreement must be accompanied by an inspection system which will enable all parties concerned to know whether the agreement is being carried out.

We must all agree that America and the free world must

maintain military strength sufficient to meet and defeat any aggressor. We do this not because we want war but because we want peace, and because history teaches us that where a potential aggressor is on the loose, weakness invites attack and strength discourages it.

With regard to the conduct of foreign policy there is a lot of disagreement—and honest disagreement, too. But it is rather easy to sit on the sidelines and say: "We are too firm and too rigid"—those charges were made against Mr. Dulles—or "We are too soft"—those charges were made against the President when he invited Mr. Khrushchev to this country. I would be the last to say that everything this Administration has done and is doing is right and therefore should be continued. But I do think this: our position of maintaining adequate military strength, combined with a diplomacy which is absolutely firm but nonbelligerent, is the only course that we can follow. Looking to the future, I am confident that if we continue to maintain such a position it will provide the best chance for bringing about an eventual change in the attitude of the Communist leaders. As long as they are convinced that we will remain firm, that we are going to maintain our defenses to protect what we have, then they may see the folly of simply continuing what has been called a balance of terror in the world. When they see that, and only then, will we be able to negotiate a reduction in the arms burden.

The basic American position is clear. We recognize that while a strong national defense serves as a deterrent to war it does not remove the possibility of a war beginning because of a miscalculation—a miscalculation arising, in turn, from the tensions existing in the world. That is why we are striving to reach an agreement for a first step which will reverse the mad and costly arms race the Soviet Union has imposed upon the free world.

We have been in the past, and are now, ready to meet the Soviet Union halfway on any reasonable basis. We are glad to note that they, now, are at least beginning to talk more reasonably than in the past.

But we owe a duty to our allies and to ourselves not to be sucked into the old shell game of trading one horse for one rabbit—which is what Mr. Khrushchev offers, in effect, when he suggests that we should withdraw our forces from Europe—3,000 miles—in return for the Soviet Union moving theirs back from the satellite countries—a mere 300 miles.

Regardless of the difficulties we confront in these negotiations we must never throw up our hands in despair. The very existence of our civilization is at stake. That is why those representing us in these negotiations deserve the united support of the American people as they explore every possible avenue which might conceivably lead to a step forward on the road to disarmament and peace.

Nor must we ever assume that disarmament on even a large scale will remove *all* danger of war. A lasting peace cannot be built on the foundation of disarmament alone. We must continue to work unceasingly to remove those basic tensions which have made the world an armed camp in the first place.

We have to recognize in our dealings with the Soviet Union —whether it is in the field of defense, at the conference table, or in economic competition—that it is going to be a long struggle. We are going to continue to have differences over a long period of time.

What we need is dedication to the pursuit of peace, which I am sure we have. But we also need stamina, and the determination that, while we are always willing to talk over our differences and search for basic solutions that do not infringe upon our national security, we will continue to stand firm for our principles.

4. *Foreign Policy in Action: Latin America* [11]

I said when I returned from Latin America in the spring of 1958 that we must not allow the unfortunate incidents that took place there to obscure the total picture of this trip. We must not allow mob action to obscure the real feeling of friendship and affection that the vast majority of the people of Latin America have for the people of the United States. There is no question in my mind that in the end the results of this trip will prove to be beneficial. But the trip will be remembered not in terms of what is said now, today, and not in terms of the stories that were written while it was going on—its success or failure will be measured in terms of what is done and what happens in the relationships between the United States and Latin America in the months and years ahead.

If, as a result, some people who may not have recognized the tremendous importance of Latin America to the United States, now realize it—the trip will have been worthwhile. If, as a result, the Latin American story, not just the story of the revolution which usually gets on the front page, but the great constructive story of a continent which is on the way to economic progress and freedom, gets from page 8 onto page 1 in the nation's great newspapers—the trip will have been worthwhile. All of these things I think should be said.

[11] The material in this section is derived from the following sources: Remarks to the American Society of Newspaper Editors, Washington, D.C. April 18, 1959. Responses to questions at the California Newspaper Publishers Association Convention, Los Angeles, California. February 6, 1960. Remarks at MATS Terminal on the return of the Vice President from his South American tour, Washington, D.C. May 15, 1958. Responses to questions at the National Press Club, Washington, D.C. May 21, 1958.

And may I say, too, that as we consider this part of the world we should realize the tremendous stake we—the United States and the free world—have in the future of Latin America. Population-wise today we are approximately equal—180 million here; 180 million there. The rate of growth in Latin American population, however, is two and one-half times as great as it is in the United States. And so by the year 2000, if the current rates of population increase continue, Latin America will have 500 million people to our own 250 million.

I should point out, also, that Latin America, next to Europe, provides the best market that the United States has. And we have other important ties: for instance the fact that in the United Nations we have stood shoulder to shoulder, time after time, on the great issues affecting the Western community, and on the principles of freedom and democracy in which all of us believe.

Despite what you may have read about my trip in 1958, as we look at the whole picture we must not forget that in the last ten years Latin America has made great economic progress. They need a great deal more, but the record in the last ten years has been encouraging.

And another area in which we find real encouragement is the steady progress in Latin American countries toward democracy and toward freedom. What has happened in Argentina, Colombia, and Venezuela, is symbolic of the progress to which I refer.

Now, let's look in detail at one of the incidents of my 1958 trip. Many people have shown particular interest in what happened in Venezuela. A full explanation, of course, would require a very long analysis.

To interpret correctly what happened in Venezuela we have to consider some much more basic problems than the violence you read about and saw through the use of the photographic medium. It would be a great mistake just to attribute what happened in Venezuela to communism. It is true that the Communists spearheaded the attack. But you have to remember that they had a lot of willing spear-carriers along with them.

Now why did this happen? We must seek beneath the surface to get at the real cause of it. There happened to exist at the time of our visit some real problems with regard to United States–Venezuelan relations. One of them was their feeling that the United States, both on the part of government and on the part of private enterprise, supported dictatorship— specifically, the dictatorship of Perez Jimenez. Another factor was the feeling in Venezuela that we had made a mistake in providing refuge for Perez Jimenez, after his overthrow, and for the former head of the Venezuelan police, Estrada.

The policy of maintaining diplomatic relations with South American nations which have various forms of dictatorial government is not a new one. It has been the policy of the United States through the years. As I have good reason to know, there is some resentment toward that policy.

It has come under attack in many South American countries. There is also some question raised about it within the United States. In our diplomatic relations with countries throughout the world, the United States generally has had and has today —and I think must continue to have—normal relations with what happens to be the government in power in those countries at a particular time.

Now this policy does not weaken in any way our own devotion to guarantees of religious freedom, freedom of the press, freedom of expression, and the other important liberties. We are devoted to freedom here. We hope that these ideas will be adopted in other countries as well. But Latin Americans, as well as free peoples everywhere, would resent nothing more than for the United States to try to tell them what kind of government they must have.

That is the reason that in promoting our policies we have had to be careful. This is particularly true in Latin America, where there is great sensitivity about the "Colossus of the north" trying to impose ideas of economics and government upon the people of the south. That is why we cannot attempt to dictate to them what kind of governments they must have or demand that their governments meet certain standards. We have attempted to encourage, where we can, those particular groups within these countries which stand for the freedoms that we think are so very important. We can and will continue to so encourage—but we cannot and will not make demands.

Another factor behind my reception in Venezuela related to economic problems. In Venezuela, which depends to a great extent as you know on its oil exports to the United States, there had been some economic decline parallel to that in the United States.

A significant fact we should remember about Venezuela is that it has experienced the greatest economic progress of any country in Latin America. Through the tremendous development of its oil resources it has been able to embark on a program of public works and some programs in the field of public housing which were astounding to all members of our party. The question which comes to the minds of observers trying to get beneath the surface is this: how is it that a country experiencing such great economic progress is the one where you had the most violent demonstrations? The great lesson for the United States, insofar as its policy toward Latin America is concerned, is that economic progress in itself is not enough.

The idea exists among many people in Latin America that when private enterprise comes to a country it means providing and sustaining a good life for the few rather than for the many. This idea exists in too many quarters.

What we must prove and what we must show is that when private enterprise comes into Latin America, when the United States comes in with its programs of assistance, Point 4, and Export-Import Bank Loans, we do so not for the purpose of simply keeping in power a group of the élite who have enjoyed a great deal of the world's goods for many, many years. We do not have in mind simply making the rich richer and the poor poorer. What we do believe is that the best way toward economic progress, to raise the living standards of the miserably poor people all over Latin America, is through a program of enlightened private enterprise combined with government assistance in those areas where private enterprise cannot do the job.

Now, all these issues were played upon by the Communists in Venezuela—played upon very effectively, and used to stir up the people, themselves non-Communists, in such a way that they would resort to violence against a visitor from abroad. And this, by the way, is completely out of character for the Venezuelan people.

I have been asked whether the Communists, who in some instances inspired the incidents which occurred, made any mistakes. I can best answer that question by pointing out what Muñoz Marin, the very capable Governor of Puerto Rico and an expert in this particular field of Communist propaganda, observed on our way back to the United States. He said: "Mr. Vice President, there were several particular incidents and actions in the various demonstrations against you which indicated they were controlled by Communists, and were not simply the action of Latin American liberals." He said that while some of their slogans were the usual ones that a Latin American liberal might use, in some instances they used slogans which were clearly those of the international Communist movement and not at all typically Latin American. For example, "Freedom for Puerto Rico" and "Freedom for Mr. Campos," the man who tried to kill Mr. Truman.

Then, too, there were the slogans with regard to the "banning of the bomb" and other international slogans which are not typically Latin American. The truth is that on most international issues, Latin Americans of all political hues, with the exception of the Communists, stand shoulder to shoulder with the United States.

The second Communist mistake Governor Muñoz Marín pointed out was the denial of freedom of speech which occurred at San Marcos University in Lima, Peru, and which also occurred as a result of the riots in Venezuela. One of the arguments that the Communists had been using against the dictatorships in Latin America, after all, was that freedom was being denied, and particularly freedom of speech. And then when this opportunity was presented them to show that they could use speech instead of resorting to violent demonstrations, they resorted to violence. By denying freedom of speech, by resorting to excesses, they exposed themselves using the very tactics that they would use if they came to power. This exposure, Governor Muñoz Marín said, actually served a useful purpose.

He also pointed out that not only did the crowds continue to conduct their demonstrations and their cat-calls during the playing of the national anthem of the United States but also when the national anthem of their own country was played. This seemed to show that they were not Venezuelan in their loyalty, not Peruvian in their loyalty, but were loyal to another system and another allegiance entirely.

If as a result, some people who did not previously recognize the true character and nature of the Communist conspiracy now recognize it, these unfortunate demonstrations will have at least served a useful purpose.

Governor Muñoz Marín pointed out another significant occurrence. He said that perhaps the greatest error the mobs made, from the standpoint of eliciting support throughout Latin America, was when they insulted Mrs. Nixon. The people of Latin America have great respect for women. A man, in politics, is fair game, but to a woman courtesy is always shown.

By insulting Mrs. Nixon these people showed that they were truly not Venezuelan, not Peruvian, in their attitudes.

I can say in that respect, with I think pardonable pride, that long after these incidents are forgotten, there will be literally thousands of people in all the eight countries we visited who will remember the visits that Mrs. Nixon paid to orphanages, to hospitals, and to various other institutions. As I have said on many previous occasions, there is no question that the Vice President is controversial; but I am happy to say that, except for a very small Communist minority, Mrs. Nixon is not controversial in Latin America.

In reference to my South American trip, some people have voiced the opinion that it is beneath the dignity of the Vice President of the United States to go around debating with radical students.

I have heard that objection raised after every trip I have taken. I have had it raised by some of our ambassadors before the debates occurred—but usually not afterward. I think this very objection points up one of the grave problems that we confront in our relations not only with Latin America but with Africa and with Asia where newly developing societies are moving toward political democracy.

There was a time in the relatively recent history of Latin America when a revolution was simply a way to transfer power from one section of the élite to another. These revolts had no popular base whatever. But when you consider what has been happening in Argentina, Colombia, and Venezuela, when you look at the new leaders who are arising on the Latin American scene—Frondizi, for example, in Argentina and Lleras in Colombia, and Siles in Bolivia—when you examine the character and background of the fine men I met in the government *junta* in Venezuela, then you see that there is emerging a new group of leaders of true mass-based revolutions.

Where do these leaders come from? These people come not from the very wealthy and the usual ruling class but from a new group, a class I call the intelligentsia.

This brings me to the key questions: why do I go to universities? why do I go, as I did in every country possible, to labor union halls?

I want to point out the format we used. First, we went only when we were invited, and the universities generally issued the invitations because they were most anxious to have the opportunity of seeing a visiting dignitary from abroad and submitting questions to him. Second, these were not debates in the usual sense. I went to the university and made a few opening comments and then submitted myself to questioning.

I will tell you why I used that format. When you do not know the language, the question-and-answer technique is far more effective than the set speech. You can punctuate your points and isolate the problems and, believe me, in these question-and-answer sessions we covered every difficult, tough problem that you could possibly imagine. The labor leaders and the university students who asked questions were not diplomats. They really wanted to get down to brass tacks.

What was the result? First, it was good for me. I learned a lot about Latin America. Second, I believe it is essential from the standpoint of American foreign policy that we talk to these groups and answer these difficult questions.

I can assure you it is a lot easier to run one of these trips the way some people want them run—a round of cocktail parties and white-tie dinners. We had a lot of those, too. But if that is what we do, exclusively, in Latin America, if we continue to concentrate primarily on the élite groups, we might as well admit right now that we are going to lose the battle. Although the people in the universities do not run these countries now, they will in the future; although the people in the universities do not control policy now, they already affect policy very directly.

The same is true of the incipient labor movements in Latin America. They are weak at present but growing stronger.

It is significant to note, in this context, that the Communists are concentrating on the universities and the labor union movements. Why? Because they know that these groups comprise the wave of the future and the Communists are trying to steer them in the communist direction. The question is: do we leave the field to the Communists or do we go in and debate these issues with this rising new force which in five or ten years is going to be a terribly important factor in Latin America and in the free world?

In instance after instance I think it was possible for me to answer some of the difficult questions about United States policy that ought to be answered. Does the United States really favor dictatorships? The answer is no. Does the United States in its private enterprise really want to make the rich richer and the poor poorer? The answer is no. Over and over again I tried to get this message across using specific instances and hard facts.

I repeat that it is easier to travel the other way. But I also repeat that in all aspects of our foreign policy activities at the diplomatic level, at the USIA level, at the economic level, it is high time we paid more attention to the university students and the rising labor leaders and the people in the press and the radio—the opinion-making people—than we have in the past. If we do not we are simply leaving the field to the other side. If I had to do it over again I would do the same thing, and I would urge any other visitors who go there to do likewise.

On my return from Latin America, it struck me that our reception there was not as bad as it may have read in the papers.

It is true that our reception was violent in the extreme in Venezuela. It could have reached similar violence in Peru. But I would point out the side of the story which perhaps has never been adequately told, and not because of any fault on the part of the newsmen. Violence makes news; controversy makes news, whereas a peaceful reception and a constructive conference end up on the back page. The story that is not told, for example, is that in Peru, in scores and scores of places that we visited, we received a very friendly welcome.

After we left the University of San Marcos we went next door—and this is a shift our friends on the other side did not expect—to the Catholic University of Lima. They did not know we were coming. I simply walked in. I stood before a group of three or four hundred students and answered questions about United States policies with regard to Peru, as I had hoped to do at San Marcos. And, as always, they were tough questions.

At the conclusion of that question period I think any objective reporter would say that the audience was overwhelmingly friendly. The next day, the crowds everywhere we went were overwhelmingly friendly. I was particularly touched by the fact that student groups, labor groups, groups from government, and people in all walks of life came to see us at the hotel and protested that mob violence was not the attitude of the great majority of the Peruvians and repeated over and over again that Peruvians were essentially friendly to the people of the United States.

In Caracas the same thing happened, although on a smaller scale, because we did not have the opportunity to move through the town. But on the day after the riots we had delegations calling on us all day long, delegations from the various women's societies calling on Mrs. Nixon, delegations from three of the universities calling on me, all of them protesting that although they had some disagreements with certain policies of the United States, they believed the use of violence toward a visitor, particularly a visitor from the United States, was completely out of character with the attitude of Venezuela.

They apologized for what had happened and then sat down for serious discussions of our mutual problems. What I am trying to say is simply this: yes, there was danger and we are fortunate nothing worse happened; but we must not let the violence obscure the more basic fact that as far as Venezuela and Peru are concerned, there is still a tremendous amount of friendship for the United States. And in all the countries we visited, I found many similar signs of a strong bond.

Since that spring of 1958, we have been making steady progress toward some of our goals. We have seen some important new avenues of economic cooperation opened through the discussions of the Organization of American States' Committee of Twenty-one. And here I think we should give due recognition to the initiative of President Kubitschek of Brazil for suggesting this "Operation Pan America."

In addition, the twenty-one American republics have now signed the final act of the Inter-American Development Bank, which, when placed in operation, will provide another source of capital for Latin American development needs. In a sense, this plan takes Latin America somewhat out of the category of the other so-called underdeveloped nations, and properly suggests that this area is to be given special consideration by the United States. In view of the special problems which are mutually theirs and ours and because of the proximity of the Latin American nations to the United States, this would appear to be an appropriate distinction.

These steps, along with measures that have been taken by many of the Latin American governments in cooperation with the international monetary funds to stabilize their internal financial situations, are positive moves designed to strengthen economies in the Western Hemisphere. I would not suggest that we have solved the economic problems faced by Latin America, but there have been possible solutions to those problems proposed, and we are making definite progress toward implementing those solutions at this time.

One other comment with regard to the problems of intervention in Latin American affairs. The recent flare-ups of tension in the Caribbean area, with reports of activities in various countries designed to overthrow the governments of other nations, emphasizes the importance of this principle of non-intervention to which we are all dedicated in the Americas.

The Organization of American States has played an outstanding role in maintaining the peace and security of the area. Each country in the Americas must be assured of the right to develop its political life, free from outside intervention. That is why the United States announced at Montevideo, twenty-six years ago, its willingness to adhere to the principle of non-intervention. That is why, in the following year, the Platt Amendment was abrogated by agreement with the government leaders of Cuba.[12]

I am confident that nothing has contributed more to the growth of freedom and democracy in this region than the steadfast devotion of the American public to the principle of non-intervention, and the United States will certainly continue to practice and preach that principle in its relations with our friends in the Americas.

Recently, there has been much concern expressed from time to time over the danger of Communism, in Cuba particularly, but also elsewhere in the American hemisphere. We are all

[12] At the time that Cuba became an independent nation, in 1901, the U.S. Congress insisted that a series of special provisions be written into the Cuban Constitution—gathered together in the so-called Platt Amendment—reserving to the United States, in effect, the right to intervene in Cuban affairs to protect American interests and property, and in behalf of American citizens. This limitation on Cuban sovereignty, long a sore-point in U.S. relations with all of Latin America, was renounced by our government in 1934. Since that time the principle of "non-intervention" has been central to our Latin American policy and has been formally adhered to by all 21 American republics.

aware that all of the countries in the hemisphere have an interest in seeing to it that this threat does not become so great that the Communists are able to dominate any government in the hemisphere. Such an interest has been traditional in the American republics since the time of the Monroe Doctrine. For communism to come to any one of the American republics is the very foreign intervention to which the Monroe Doctrine referred. For this reason, in our discussion with the leaders of other countries in this hemisphere, we can honestly say that we are speaking in their interest when we urge that they join us in resisting any Communist infiltration which might result in control of any government.

In Latin America we are dealing with an area which is, in a sense, in a state of evolution; the people there are primarily concerned—as they should be—about the poverty and misery and disease which still exists in so many places. They are determined to do something about it. They are moving toward democracy and freedom—sometimes slowly, but without question surely. They are moving toward economic progress. And the United States is, and should be, proud to work with them as partners in moving toward democracy, toward freedom, and toward economic progress.

Since 1953 we have seen changes in Argentina, Colombia, and other countries in South America, from dictatorship to some degree of freedom and some degree of representative government. These changes have come about without outside interference.

When I returned from Latin America in 1958 I expressed my view of the proper attitude of the United States to these changes in this way: in our relations with countries that have forms of government that we may find unattractive or repugnant, we should have a proper relationship—a handshake, you might call it. For the kind of governments that guarantee the freedoms that we think are so important, we should have an *embrazo*—a warm embrace. This must be done bearing in mind the basic idea that the United States must not interfere or give any appearance of interfering with these people or imposing our form of government upon them. I think this is a sound position, one that in the end will be successful in promoting the evolution in Latin America toward more representative government and away from dictatorship.

One rule we must never forget in international relations, as well as in all political and business affairs, is that we must never take our friends for granted. What we must get across to our friends in Latin America, as well as in other parts of the world, is this very simple message: we, the government and people of the United States, want for other people just what we have for ourselves—independence for our country, freedom for our people, and the greatest possibilities for economic progress that can be devised; the only war the people of the United States want to wage is a war against poverty, misery, and disease, wherever they exist in the world.

5. *Foreign Policy in Action: Africa* [13]

On the basis of my visit to Africa—specifically to Morocco, Ghana, Liberia, Uganda, Ethiopia, Sudan, Libya, and Tunisia —I made the following observations and submit the following recommendations.

No one can travel in Africa, even as briefly as I did, without realizing the tremendous potentialities of this great continent. Africa is the most rapidly changing area in the world today. The course of its development, as its people continue to emerge

[13] The material in this section is derived from "The Emergence of Africa," the Vice President's Report to the President on his trip to Africa, March 21, 1957.

from a colonial status and assume the responsibilities of independence and self-government,[14] could well prove to be the decisive factor in the world-wide conflict between the forces of freedom and international communism.

The leaders and people of the countries I visited in Africa have many things in common. They cherish their independence, which most of them have only recently acquired, and are determined to protect it against any form of foreign domination. They rightfully expect recognition from us and others of their dignity and equality as individuals and peoples in the family of nations. They want progress for their undeveloped economies.

The great question which is presented to the leaders of Africa is whether they can attain these justifiable objectives and at the same time develop and maintain governmental institutions based on principles of freedom and democracy. I believe they all are convinced that they can, and I am dead sure that the free world has a vital interest in assisting them to do so. For the success or failure of these new members of the family of nations to realize their aspirations in this manner will have profound effects upon the development of Africa and on the world in the years just ahead.

Herein lies the wider significance of the emergence of a new nation like Ghana. The eyes of the peoples of Africa south of the Sahara, and of Western Europe too, will be upon this new state to see whether the orderly transition which has taken place from dependent to independent status, and whether the retention of close ties on a basis of equality with the British

[14] Just since 1957, when this report was written, the roll-call of new African nations is impressive: in 1958, Guinea achieved independence; this year, seven new nations will be added—Cameroon, Togoland, the Belgian Congo, the Mali Federation, Somalia, Madagascar, and Nigeria. Both the Federation of Rhodesia and Nyasaland, and Sierre Leone, are well on their way toward independence in the early '60s. By the end of this year, in fact, 180 million of Africa's 240 million people will be self-governing.

Commonwealth, will continue to work successfully. If it does, we may have here a formula of possible application in other cases. By the same token, inimical forces will be closely following the situation to see whether any openings present themselves for exploitation, in order to disrupt and destroy the independence which Ghana seeks to achieve.

Nor is this situation peculiar to Ghana. The same factors are present everywhere among the independent states I visited. Africa is emerging as one of the great forces in the world today. In a world in which, because of advances in technology, the influence of ideas and principles is becoming increasingly important in the battle for men's minds and allegiance, we in the United States must come to know, to understand, and to find common ground with the peoples of this great continent. It is in this context that my recommendations are presented.

Africa is producing great leaders, dedicated to the principles of independence, world responsibility, and the welfare of their people. Such men as the Sultan of Morocco, Prime Minister Nkrumah of Ghana, President Tubman of Liberia, the Emperor of Ethiopia, and Prime Ministers Abdullah Khalil of the Sudan, Ben Halim of Libya, and Habib Bourguiba of Tunisia, certainly compare most favorably with the great leaders of the world. These are all men who command respect beyond the borders of their own countries. They are backed up by other equally dedicated leaders who have much to contribute both to the problems of their own countries and to those which plague the world today.

The United States must come to know these leaders better, to understand their hopes and aspirations, and to support them in their plans and programs for strengthening their own nations and contributing to world peace and stability. To this end, we must encourage the greatest possible interchange of persons and ideas with the leaders and peoples of these countries. We must assure the strongest possible diplomatic and consular representation to these countries and stand ready to consult them as equals on all matters affecting their interests and ours.

There is no area in the world today in which the prestige of the United States is more uniformly high than in the countries I visited on this trip. The President is respected as the acknowledged leader of the free world. There is a most encouraging understanding of our programs and policies. These countries know that we have no ambitions to dominate them and that the cornerstone of our foreign policy is to assist all countries in resisting outside domination. They understand that the United States stands on principle and that this was the motivating force, for example, which led us to act as we did in the Suez crisis. They approve the stand which we took at that time and look confidently to us to act similarly in the future. They understand that the Eisenhower Doctrine is dedicated to the principle of assisting the states of the Middle East to maintain their independence.[15] They know that the United States stands for the evolution of dependent peoples toward self-government and independence, as they become able to discharge the responsibilities of nationhood.

This understanding of the principles for which we stand as a nation is a tremendous asset to us in this area. The maintenance of our present high prestige in Africa will depend upon whether the people of the continent continue to understand our dedication to the principles of independence, equality,

[15] In January 1957, President Eisenhower requested that Congress pass a special resolution authorizing U.S. intervention in Middle Eastern nations (a) on request of the legal government (b) when threatened by overt aggression or by internal subversion, directed and supported by external power. Congress passed such a resolution—the so-called Eisenhower Doctrine—in March 1957 and it was first invoked in July 1958 when, following the Iraqi revolution, the government of Lebanon appealed for direct U.S. military aid against the threat of violent internal revolt. U.S. troops were sent, and later promptly withdrawn, as requested.

and economic progress to which they themselves are so deeply devoted. We must staff our diplomatic and information establishments in these countries with men and women capable of interpreting and explaining our policies and actions.

As a result of skillful propaganda primarily inspired by the enemies of freedom, however, a consistently distorted picture of the treatment of minority races in the United States is being effectively presented in the countries I visited. Every instance of prejudice in this country is blown up in such manner as to create a completely false impression of the attitudes and practices of the great majority of the American people. The result is irreparable damage to the cause of freedom, which is at stake. We must continue to strike at the roots of this problem. We cannot talk equality to the peoples of Africa and Asia and practice inequality in the United States. In the national interest, as well as for the moral issue involved, we must support the necessary steps which will assure orderly progress toward the elimination of discrimination in the United States. And we should do a far more effective job than we are presently doing, in Africa and elsewhere, in telling the true story of the real progress that is being made toward realizing this objective.

All the African states which I visited are underdeveloped. Most of them have great economic potential. Their leaders are anxious to strengthen the economies of their countries in order to assure for their peoples a larger share of the advantages of our modern civilization. They seek economic as well as political independence insofar as this is possible in today's world.

Their needs are great in the fields of education and public health. They require roads and other communications in order to open inaccessible territories to economic development. They need agricultural development to sustain their expanding populations. They want assistance in developing their great mineral and forest resources. They foresee great opportunities for developing small industrial enterprises. In most cases, these developmental needs are beyond their capacity to finance.

All of the leaders with whom I talked expressed preference for developing their economies through encouraging the investment of private capital and through loans from international agencies such as the World Bank where feasible, rather than through government-to-government grants. It can truly be said that the welcome sign is out for investment of foreign private capital in Africa. African leaders are aware of the great role that such private capital can play in the development of their countries and many of them have adopted, or are in the process of adopting, special legislation designed to create an atmosphere conducive to expanded foreign investment.

The United States government should, through appropriate agencies, draw the attention of private American capital to opportunities for investment in those areas where the conditions for such investment are propitious. Strengthening the economic sections of American embassies in this area is especially needed if this objective is to be carried out.

We should support applications before the appropriate international agencies for financing sound economic development projects in the area.

To the extent that our resources and the demands of other areas permit, we should extend economic and technical assistance to the countries of Africa, helping them to further their economic development.

In this connection, I think it is appropriate to place in proper context the United States economic assistance programs. A comment on what has happened in Italy may be pertinent. While my visit to Italy was not on an official basis, I did have the opportunity to discuss economic and political problems with President Gronchi, Prime Minister Segni, and other Italian officials. It was significant to me that at the time I arrived in Italy, the last American aid office was being closed. I recalled that ten years before when I visited Italy as a member of the Herter Committee on Foreign Aid,[16] the most dire predictions were being made as to the future of the Italian economy. It was said in the United States that American assistance would be thrown down a rat hole, that the Italian people should live within their own means, that they should work harder, and that in any event, once the economic program began, we would never see the end of it. The fact that Italy today has one of the soundest, most productive economies in Europe is eloquent proof of the validity of economic assistance properly administered and properly used by the recipient country.

While the economic problems of Italy were obviously different from those Africa now faces, I am confident that in the African countries I visited we shall have similar success as we work in cooperation with their enlightened leaders toward the development of their great natural and human resources.

Africa is a priority target for the international Communist movement. I received the distinct impression that the Communists consider Africa today to be as important in their designs for world conquest as they considered China to be twenty-five years ago. Consequently, they are mounting a massive diplomatic, propaganda, and economic offensive in all parts of the continent. They are trying desperately to convince the peoples of Africa that they support more strongly than we do their natural aspirations for independence, equality, and economic progress.

Fortunately, their efforts thus far have not been generally

---

[16] In 1947, as a freshman Congressman, the Vice President was appointed to the Select Committee on Foreign Aid (the Herter Committee, so-called for its chairman, Christian Herter, then Congressman from Massachusetts) which conducted an on-the-spot study of American economic aid programs in Western Europe during the summer of 1947. The Vice President and other of the Committee members were subsequently instrumental in arousing public and Congressional support for a sustained effort in the field of mutual security.

successful and, for the present, Communist domination is not an imminent danger. All of the African leaders to whom I talked are determined to maintain their independence against communism or any other form of foreign domination. They have taken steps to bring under control the problem of Communist subversion of their political, economic, and social life. It would be a great mistake, however, to be complacent about this situation; the Communists are without question putting their top men in the fields of diplomacy, intrigue, and subversion into the African area to probe for openings which they can exploit for their own selfish and disruptive ends.

The Communist threat underlines the wisdom and necessity of our assisting the countries of Africa to maintain their independence and to alleviate the conditions of want and instability on which communism breeds. The importance of Africa to the strength and stability of the free world is too great for us to underestimate or to become complacent about this danger without taking every step within our power to assist these countries to maintain their effective independence.

In every instance where my schedule permitted, I made it a point to talk to the chief labor leaders. I was encouraged to find that the free trade union movement is making great advances in Africa, particularly in Ghana, Morocco, and Tunisia. The union leaders of these countries have recognized the importance of providing an alternative to Communist-dominated unions and thereby they are keeping the Communists from getting a foothold in one of their favorite areas of exploitation. In this connection, I wish to pay tribute to the effective support that is being given by trade unions in the United States to the free trade union movement in Africa. These close and mutually advantageous relationships are very much in the national interest.

It is vitally important that the United States government follow closely African trade union developments and that our diplomatic and consular representatives should come to know on an intimate basis the trade union leaders in these countries. American labor unions should continue to maintain close fraternal relationships with the African free trade union movement in order that each may derive the greatest possible advantage from the wisdom and experience of the other.

The Nile is one the world's greatest international rivers. Perhaps in no other part of the world are the economies of so many states tied to a particular waterway. The river is so located geographically that whatever projects are undertaken on it within the territorial domains of one state are bound to have their effect on the economies of other states. The United States must take into account the common interests of the riparian states in the development of this great river and, at such time as political conditions permit, should support a cooperative approach to its development which would accord with the common interests of all the states involved.

In general, I found that our political, economic, and information programs in the countries I visited are being administered in accordance with our obligations to the American taxpayer. There is, however, always room for improvement and, in the spirit of constructive criticism, I wish to make the following public recommendations.

On the political side, I believe that our diplomatic and consular missions are generally understaffed. We must assure that these establishments have sufficient personnel to enable them to interpret our policies, to consult fully with the local governments on matters of mutual interest, and to report on developments of importance to the United States. Our diplomatic and consular officers must have sufficient funds to enable them to travel about the vast territories within their jurisdiction, for the purpose of reporting on developments outside the major centers of population and of forming contacts with the peoples of those areas. The posts in this area are, in many instances, unhealthy and trying climatically to those raised in a temperate zone. We must, therefore, try to ameliorate hardship conditions for our personnel in order that they can more effectively perform their tasks. We must recognize that the importance of the African area and the difficult living conditions there necessitate our assigning officials of the highest possible competence and stability. The emphasis should be on youth, vigor, and enthusiasm.

Insofar as our economic programs are concerned, I believe that our technicians in the field are doing an excellent job in working alongside and teaching the African. Obviously, the maintenance and support of these technicians in the field require a headquarters staff in the national capitals. From my own observations, I believe these headquarters staffs sometimes tend to become inflated and therefore I recommend that they be carefully reviewed to see whether economies in personnel could not be effected. Also, there is sometimes a tendency to scatter programs over a number of fields of economic and social development, whereas greater concentration on a few key projects might bring more lasting returns. Our program should constantly be reviewed from this point of departure.

On the informational side, I believe that the most worthwhile projects are the libraries and reading rooms which we have established in a number of centers overseas, and the exchange of persons programs. The funds available for these programs in the African area should be substantially increased over the present level.

To the extent that the Africans become familiar with the culture and technology, the ideals and aspirations and the traditions and institutions which combine to make up the American character, we shall have made great advances in common understanding. This can be done through books and periodicals, through student exchanges, and through the leader grant program for bringing outstanding Africans to the United States for study and travel. We should also assist insofar as we can, the development of indigenous educational facilities in Africa. In this way, we can get to know them and they to know us.

I believe that the information output from our radio and news programs in the African area have in the past not been as effective as they should be if we are adequately to counter the propaganda being disseminated by the Communists. In the studies which are currently being made of these programs by the USIA, I believe it is important that the highest priority be assigned to this area, both in improving the quality of personnel in the field and in providing more information which is particularly suited to the special problems of Africa.

For too many years, Africa in the minds of many Americans has been regarded as a remote and mysterious continent which was the special province of big-game hunters, explorers, and motion-picture makers. For such an attitude to exist among the public at large could greatly prejudice the maintenance of our position in the world, because the emergence of a free and independent Africa is as important to us in the long run as it is to the people of that continent.

It is for this reason that I strongly support the creation within the Department of State of a new Bureau of African Affairs which will place this continent on the some footing as the other great area groupings of the world.[17] I recommend similar action by the ICA and USIA. These bureaus, properly staffed and with sufficient funds, will better equip us to handle our relationships with the countries of Africa. But this in itself will not be enough. There must be a corresponding realization

[17] This recommendation was subsequently presented to Congress and approved. In August 1958, therefore, a Bureau of African Affairs was established in the Department of State, directed by an Assistant Secretary, on the same administrative level as the other major regional desks.

throughout the executive branches of the government, throughout the Congress, and not least, throughout the nation—a realization of the growing importance of Africa to the future of the United States and the free world and of the necessity of assigning the highest priority to our relations with that area.

6. *Foreign Policy in Action: Lebanon* [18]

The events of July 14, 1958, marked a turning point in the struggle between the forces of imperialistic communism and the forces of freedom: on that date the President of the United States ordered American troops into Lebanon.

The President had the constitutional power to do what he did. He moved American forces into Lebanon at the request of a constitutionally elected President with the unanimous approval of the cabinet of that country. He sent troops there for two purposes: one, to strengthen that government in its efforts to resist forces within the country which were stimulated and materially assisted by forces outside the country to overthrow the duly elected government; and, two, to protect the 2,500 Americans who were living in Lebanon.

The legal basis for his action is clear. But we are not concerned here simply with its legality. We are concerned with the merits. What are the prospects for the future? Was the judgment of the President of the United States, and of those of his advisers who supported his judgment, correct?

At the outset we must recognize that this was a terribly difficult decision. The situation was not black or white. As is usually the case in considering difficult problems in the international

[18] The material in this section is derived from "The Near East Situation," from a speech at the Annual Aquatennial Luncheon for Minnesota Editors, Minneapolis, Minnesota. July 19, 1958.

field, there were substantial gray areas in which the decision-makers simply had to take one course or another—either one of which had many potential dangers.

Some people have asked, for instance, why it was that when Lebanese President Chamoun asked for help, instead of moving in United States troops we did not immediately take the case to the United Nations. Why did we not ask them to send the necessary forces into Lebanon to give that government the stability and the strength it needed to resist the indigenous revolting forces that were supported from outside the country?

The answer is a very practical one. We would have preferred to follow this course of action. If we had thought that submitting the problem to the United Nations would have resulted in action quick and forceful enough to deal with the situation, we would have done just that.

We decided on another course—submitting the problem to the United Nations, but at the same time moving our own forces in as President Chamoun had requested. We did so for the practical reason that our intelligence information indicated there was a very substantial chance that if we did not move quickly, Lebanon would go the way of Iraq. Furthermore, Jordan, into which the British had moved, would likewise have gone the way of Iraq.[19] If we had waited through the discussion which must necessarily take place in the United Nations before it can take action, it might have been too late.

Another very pertinent question was raised: "What is the difference between our action in Lebanon, which this Administration undertook, and the British, French, and Israeli action in Suez, which this Administration condemned?"

[19] On July 14, 1958, the government of Iraq was violently overthrown, the king and prime minister murdered, in a coup led by General Kassem and a dissident officers' group. The governments of Lebanon and Jordan, fearing the same fate, immediately requested U.S. and U.K. military support, respectively. Both nations responded at once; their forces were later withdrawn when the immediate danger had passed.

Simply stated, the difference between the two situations is this: the action in Suez was in contravention and violation of the United Nations Charter, while our action in Lebanon was in accordance with the Charter's Article 51, providing for collective security.

In Suez, the British, the French, and the Israelis were using force as an instrument of national policy against the will of the nation which was invaded. On the other hand, the forces of the United States were invited into Lebanon by a constitutionally elected government for the purpose of assisting it to resist forces which threatened to overthrow it.

Others asked how we could distinguish the situation in Hungary from the situation in Lebanon. At first glance there would appear to be some similarities that might be embarrassing to us. At the time of the Hungarian uprising the Soviet Union said: "We were invited in by the Kadar government to assist it in suppressing the revolt." And, of course, we say we were invited in by the Lebanese government.

But there is a very great difference. We did not go into Lebanon for the purpose of dominating or controlling the government or the Lebanese people. We went there for the purpose of helping them to maintain rather than destroy their independence and their national integrity. The Soviet Union went into Hungary for the clear purpose of maintaining control from Moscow of the Hungarian puppet government.

The proof of this basic difference of intent lies in the fact that, in Hungary, the Soviet Union moved in with every intention of staying. On the other hand, we made it clear from the outset that once the United Nations was able to take action and develop the forces necessary to maintain stability and protect the territorial and governmental integrity of Lebanon, we would get out. And that is just what we did.

Another question raised by many people who were concerned with our action was whether we were getting ourselves into the position of intervening in what was strictly, in substance, a civil war.

Indeed, this was one of the most difficult aspects of the decision we had to make. As we looked at the situation in Lebanon, we could not say that those who opposed the government of President Chamoun were all Communists. Nor could we say that they were all agents of the United Arab Republic. We could not say that there were not, in the dissident forces in Lebanon, some people who were anti-Nasser, some who were anti-Communist, some who were opposed to the government on other grounds altogether.

On the other hand, when we examined the contention that here we had only a civil war, we had to find out how this civil war had been started, and how it reached such proportions that President Chamoun felt he had to have outside help to deal with it.

And here we found a solid block of evidence—125 instances of intervention in which arms and other war materials were poured into Lebanon for the rebel forces from across the Syrian border. Nor is there any question about the deliberately provocative character of the radio broadcasts, both from Egypt and from Syria, in which the rebels in Lebanon were urged to overthrow the government of President Chamoun.

If this was a civil war, then, it was a civil war which had been stimulated and fomented by forces outside the country.

How can this statement be reconciled with the report from the United Nations Commission to the effect that there was no evidence of substantial movements across the border from Syria into Lebanon of materials of war?

I do not question that the United Nations findings were honestly made, but we have to recognize, first, that they had a relatively small group to check the border. More important, those who were moving material across the border naturally would have stopped the flow once the United Nations people moved in. What happened was that the arms had flowed in before the United Nations Commission arrived and reported that, as of that time, there was no substantial flow.

I would like to turn now to a more fundamental consideration. I think we all recognize that our action in Lebanon and the British action in Jordan constituted no solution of the basic problems of the Middle East. Such action is at best a stopgap. At best it gave us the time needed to attack these more basic problems.

We realized that the Lebanon situation was fraught with great difficulties. A case could be made for the fact that we were dealing here primarily with Arab nationalism, a force which is not going to be stopped simply by sending in forces to uphold the government in power. There were other factors which complicated the situation—the feeling of the Arab countries with regard to the problem of Arab refugees, the problems of Israel and Algeria, and countless others.

Why, then, did we act, in light of these complications? The answer is that there was no acceptable alternative.

We have already examined the alternative of leaving the task entirely to the United Nations.

Let us suppose that we had done nothing. In my opinion, had we failed to respond when President Chamoun asked us to come in, our refusal to come to the aid of a government that had been friendly to the United States would have struck fear, consternation, and even panic into the hearts of the friends of the United States—not only in the Near East but all over the world. It was necessary for the United States to show that when the chips were down, despite the risk of war, we would stand by our friends.

Also, we had to consider the possibility that a chain reaction could have set in as a result of the Iraqi coup. If coups had taken place in Jordan and in Lebanon, as we think they would have, then Morocco, Tunisia, Libya, the Sudan, Saudi Arabia, Iran, even Pakistan, would have been in a very shaky position.

Let us remember Korea—they said this was a civil war, North Koreans fighting South Koreans. They said the same thing about China—Communist Chinese fighting Nationalist Chinese. They said the same thing about Viet Nam—Communist Viet Nam fighting Vietnamese. They said the same thing about Greece in 1947 and about Czechoslovakia when the *coup d'état* overthrew the free government of that country.

The enemies of freedom—the international Communist movement—have developed a new and extremely effective way of carrying out their imperialistic designs and of taking over countries. They don't go over borders as the imperialists of the past did with their armies. They go under them—under them with subversion. They stimulate and foment in country after country the forces that will overthrow the existing government.

If the free world is unable or lacks the will to develop a method for meeting this indirect aggression in which governments are overthrown from within because of outside support, the United States, along with the rest of the world, will inevitably lose its independence and freedom no matter how great its military strength.

That is why I say these two almost simultaneous events in the Middle East—in Lebanon and Jordan—may have marked a turning point in history. The United States and Great Britain, in effect, said a halt must be called—even if it meant risking retaliation by the Soviet Union—to this insidious tactic of indirect aggression.

The most basic consideration of all is what we have in mind for the future. Our planning and our policies must be based on the realization that deep in the hearts and minds of literally millions of people in the Near East and the Far East, in Africa and also Latin America, is a desire for change. Because of this dissatisfaction with the status quo, those who come to them supporting their desire for change obtain tremendous support, particularly among the leaders in the intellectual communities who can effect the overturn of a government and who can help to stimulate such mob violence as we saw in Iraq.

The leaders of the Soviet Union have played on this tremendous desire for change. They have associated themselves in nation after nation with those elements that want change. Although we know full well that the Soviet Union would not bring the kind of change that these people want, the local people do not know it.

Our major problem in the years ahead, then, is to develop more effective information and economic aid programs which will identify American policy with the legitimate aspirations of these peoples.

These aspirations are, first and above all, national independence and recognition of their dignity and equality as nations and individuals; second, but still important, economic progress; and third, individual freedom.

There is no question but that this is exactly what we want for ourselves, and what we believe United States policy is designed to provide and encourage for others. But this message has not been adequately transmitted to the world.

We hear a great deal today about the threat of the Communist revolution, as well we should. But I would suggest that we can better project ourselves to the peoples of the world, particularly in those areas to which I have referred, by talking more about the promise of the American Revolution than the threat of the Communist revolution. Let us never forget that it was the American Revolution that caught the imagination of the world nearly two centuries ago.

We stood then for independence for all nations, however small, for economic progress, and for freedom. We stand for the same things today.

Our objective must be to convince people everywhere that the United States and those with whom we are associated are the protagonists of the real, the true revolution, that which matches progress with freedom.

This is our problem, and our opportunity, for the years ahead.

7. Foreign Policy in Action: Communist China [20]

Time and again over the past eight years, the critics of the present Administration have claimed that we have been too rigid in insisting on a firm stand against recognition of Red China. The question is often put, "Considering our policy toward some other dictatorships, should we not adopt a different attitude toward Red China? By recognizing Red China, might we not influence its conduct of foreign policy in the future?"

I recognize—looking ahead over the next twenty-five years—that it is essential that we in the West take the long view on all of these problems. What happens in Communist China is going to have a great impact on the retention of freedom and the maintenance of peace throughout the world.

Looking at the problem at the present time, however, my position with regard to being able to influence the course of Red China's development can be expressed in two ways. First let us consider the example of our British friends: they recognize Red China. Their relations with Red China have not improved at all by reason of recognition and are no better than ours. So I doubt that we should take the naïve attitude that by

[20] The material in this section is derived from the following sources:

Responses to questions at the California Newspaper Publishers Association Convention, Los Angeles, California. February 6, 1960. Responses to questions at Televised Press Conference, Los Angeles Press Club, Los Angeles, California. February 18, 1958. Responses to questions at the Conference with Representatives of the Four Armed Services, Washington, D.C. July 29, 1957.

recognizing Red China and elevating them to the status of a respected member of the community of nations, we are thereby going to get better treatment from the Red Chinese at a time when their policies are obviously aggressive—much more so, as a matter of fact, than those of the Soviet Union.

Secondly, let us look at this problem from the standpoint of American and free world foreign policy. I can think of nothing which would be more detrimental to the cause of freedom and peace to which we are dedicated than to recognize Red China and admit it to the United Nations at this time.

The Charter of the United Nations states unequivocally that it is an organization of peace-loving nations or nations dedicated to peace. The question immediately arises, how did the Soviet Union get in? They were, of course, charter members. As far as Red China is concerned, at a time when they are engaged in aggressive activities in Tibet, when they are engaged in activities against a United Nations member, India, in a border dispute, when they are still in defiance of the United Nations in Korea, when their policy is directed openly toward subversion in every free country in Asia—I think to reward this kind of conduct by recognition and admission to the United Nations would have a disastrous effect throughout Asia, and for that reason cannot now be considered as a real possibility.

Now, this is a position which I know could very well be at issue during the course of the 1960 campaign. But I feel that under present circumstances, when you study all the facets of the problem and see what effect recognition would have, the conclusion has to be that our present policy of nonrecognition must be continued.

As long as Red China maintains, as it has in the past, and as it does at the present, a position of defiance to the United Nations by its actions in Korea, in Indo-China, and in other parts of the world, we would be making a mistake to recognize that government in any way. And I mean not only diplomatically but also through such *de facto* recognition as is involved in cultural exchanges.

The moment that we elevate the Red Chinese regime to the position of respected member of the family of nations, what do we suppose is going to happen? The impact of such an action throughout Asia might well be catastrophic as far as our interests are concerned.

We often hear the term "overseas Chinese." There are not too many of them, compared to the number of people in Red China itself—where there are some 550 to 600 million.

There are only about 12 million so-called overseas Chinese. But let's see where they are.

There are 3 million in Indonesia. There are 3 million in Malaya, and another 2 million in Thailand. And there are a great number, pretty close to a million, in the Philippines. There are also overseas Chinese in Burma.

Now what would happen to them in the event that Communist China became a recognized member of the family of nations in good standing? These overseas Chinese would then owe their allegiance to this Communist government and there would be set in motion in all of these countries—all of which of course are trying to maintain their independence—subversive activities which might result in just the imbalance that would push them over to the Communist side and away from the side of the free nations.

From time to time in recent years, I have been asked whether conditions in Communist China might not be changing for the better. To attempt to answer such a question, I can only guess, because of course I have never been to Red China and it is one area where our intelligence is not too reliable. Nor do I claim any special knowledge on this score.

It would seem to me, however, that there are no grounds at the moment for any immediate hope of a revolution in Red China.

I would like to believe the contrary. I do think that they

are having trouble in Red China—economic troubles, especially. Agriculturally, for example, production is not what it should be or what it was once claimed to be. I think they are having political troubles, too—differences of views and opinions. But basically I think we have to assume that Red China is still under the iron control of a few men at the top, and that it will remain so, at least for an indefinite time.

Occasionally some specific event or announcement made by the Chinese—for example, their offer in 1958 to withdraw their troops from North Korea—might suggest to some a fundamental change in their policies.

I personally do not see in these moves any significant changes on which we can base a change in our own policy. As far as the offer of withdrawing troops from North Korea is concerned, I do not see that that offer is one that will pave the way for any reduction of tensions in that area. As a matter of fact, what is needed in the Korean situation, as we all know, is simply an agreement to conduct free elections; the Red Chinese and the North Koreans have consistently refused to agree to that. In evaluating such announcements, we must consider whether they involve deeds which would really reduce tension, or merely words which are designed, primarily, for propaganda consumption. I think the offer of withdrawal of troops was a propaganda venture.

With these factors in mind, we must continue to remain firm in our attitude toward Communist China. Will our policies ever change? The answer is: they will change, but only when the policies of the Communist Chinese government change.

We must expect in the years ahead that there will be changes in Red China. But, until we find a real and significant change in their policy toward the free world, we and our allies must continue on our present course.

There is a considerable body of opinion in the world that sees a split developing between Red China and the Soviet

Union, and believes that the policies of the United States and the other free nations should be designed to encourage that split. Eventually, according to this view, we would not have this tremendous force of manpower in Red China, together with the industrial power of the Soviet Union, joined together in a united bloc against the free world.

If such a split were actually developing and if it were something that we could anticipate reaching culmination in the near future, this line of reasoning would certainly stand up.

I am inclined to think, however, that at the present time this prospect is, in essence, wishful thinking. I realize there are experts in this field who disagree. Nevertheless, this is my opinion.

I believe that the Soviet Union and Red China today can be classed in all essentials as partners, with the same *major* objectives. They both want, of course, to impose the Communist system on their own peoples, and they are both dedicated to the eventual success of the Communist world revolution. And they will work together toward that overriding goal.

At the present time the Soviet Union is the senior partner and will continue to be as long as its strength is greater than that of Red China. I believe that the partnership will be held together not by any personal friendships between the leaders —and, by the same token, that means that the partnership will not be destroyed by mere personal animosities between them— but by their common adherence to and belief in the Marxist, Leninist, and Stalinist theories.

Now I use the word Stalinist advisedly, recognizing that Mr. Khrushchev has said some things about Stalin that are far from complimentary. And also Mao Tse-tung has said some things which would indicate that he is taking a different line in Communist China, in this as in other respects, from the one they are taking in the Soviet Union.

But when you analyze what has been done in these countries and you look at it over the long range, I think you can reach only one conclusion: at least in the foreseeable future, and until we have much more solid evidence to the contrary, we must continue to assume that the Soviet Union and Communist China will be working together toward the same major goal of world domination. And since they are working together, our own policies must be designed to meet the common threat they present.

PART FOUR

Democracy at Work

1. *Politics and Leadership* [21]

The word politics causes some people lots of trouble. Let us be very clear—politics is not a dirty word. It should, in fact, be the part-time job of every American. Without citizen participation in politics, self-government inevitably degenerates into anarchy or dictatorship. Actually, bad politics and bad government are caused by good citizens who do not bother to take an active interest by voting and working in the political party of their choice.

The businessman, the student, the American in every walk of life should choose the party that comes closest to his political beliefs and ideas, roll up his sleeves, and go to work. He should make his voice heard in that party. No one achieves a thing by standing on the sidelines wringing his hands and wondering why someone does not do something about a problem that directly affects him. And nowadays almost every problem of government affects almost every citizen.

[21] The material in this section is derived from the following sources:
Remarks at the 1960 Founders' Day Program, University of Nebraska, Lincoln, Nebraska. March 28, 1960. Remarks at the Dinner of the Republican State Committee for the District of Columbia, Washington, D.C. April 10, 1959. Responses to questions at News Conference, Miami Beach, Florida. January 16, 1960. Responses to questions at the California Newspaper Publishers Association Convention, Los Angeles, California. February 6, 1960. Responses to questions at News Conference, Detroit, Michigan. February 15, 1960. Remarks at Salute to Republicans Dinner, New York, New York. January 20, 1958. Filmed Remarks by Vice President Richard M. Nixon for the Syracuse Practical Politics Seminars. February 3, 1958. Televised Press Conference, Los Angeles Press Club, Los Angeles, California. February 18, 1958. Remarks to Members of the Republican National Committee, Washington, D.C. June 6, 1957. Remarks at the Ninety-ninth Annual Commencement, Michigan State University, East Lansing, Michigan. June 9, 1957. Statement by the Vice President. September 27, 1958.

I believe that every American should make a personal and lifetime commitment to take an active part in the political life of his community.

Some must run for office. No individual should avoid his responsibility in this respect with the excuse that politics is a dirty business. If he believes it is, all the more reason to get into the thick of it and do something about cleaning it up.

We need seasoned and practical leaders of the business community in politics, as well as the younger men and women of industry, too.

Those who do not make politics a career can participate on a volunteer basis in the activities of their party. Both of our major parties can use new blood and new leadership.

All citizens can help create the intelligent and informed public opinion which is essential if a democracy is to survive. The two most dangerous enemies of successful democratic government are ignorance and prejudice. And steering clear of politics breeds both these evils.

Doctors, lawyers, teachers, engineers, businessmen, homemakers—all of us, in fact, are sometimes tempted to adopt the attitude: Why borrow trouble? Why take a position on controversial issues? And if you have to take a stand, always support what appears to be the popular side of the question.

Today we must not fall into that error. We must have the courage to take firm and clear positions on the great issues of our time, and in doing so, we must not let a Gallup poll make up our minds for us. What may be the easy or popular answer to a hard question may not always be the right one. And the man who believes that what appears to be an unpopular position is the right one should make it his business to make it the popular one. Remember this: politics is in essence the driving force of our American system of self-government.

Let me make another point clear. We must not think of politics as primarily a national or even a state situation, far removed from the individual. Elections are not won in Washington, D.C., or in state capitals. National elections are simply the sum of local elections in the 3,000 counties of our nation. The basis of good politics, then, begins in the thousands of precincts in America—right down in the neighborhood. President Eisenhower summed it up when he said: "In our effort to keep the kind of government we want, you citizens are on the political front lines—the precincts of America. . . . Only through your efforts will we continue to have the kind of America all of us so earnestly desire."

Let us consider just one very practical and obvious application of politics—so much a part of our social order, in fact, that we tend to take it for granted.

That is the problem of political succession.

In a country that has no "politics"—a Communist country, for example—this problem is almost continuously explosive. There is always an undercurrent of bitter struggle and uncertainty, the threat of violent and unpredictable change. Communist regimes are preeminently governments not of laws but of men —a particular group of men who at any given moment have the upper hand in the power struggle.

In this country we know exactly when a President's term will end and exactly what procedures will be followed to designate his successor. We respect the procedures for determining political succession, and no matter how intense the rivalry may be we abide by the decisions registered in free elections. These procedures are protected by the laws of our country—laws existing for the sake of guaranteeing honest adoption of the decisions of American voters. These decisions themselves are the outcome of political contests. Without politics there could be no freedom.

It is time that we Americans recognize that the art of politics is not only necessary but desirable—indeed, that it is absolutely essential—if a free country is to keep pace with the times. The secret of America's growth is competition. This is true in business and it is also true in politics. Healthy competition between our two great political parties produces better candidates and better programs than they otherwise would present. Win or lose, we serve the nation when we contribute to and work for the party of our choice.

I happen to be a Republican. I believe that our party can best meet the challenge of the future because of our dedication to the principle of freedom—for the individual, for our economy, and for every aspect of our national life.

But neither political party has a monopoly on honesty, on patriotism, or on devotion to the basic objectives all Americans share—keeping our country strong, our people prosperous, and the world at peace.

America today cannot settle for anything less than the best leadership the nation can produce. The competition between our parties has been in the past and will continue to be in the future the most effective means for finding the best leaders and the best policies for the nation.

There is understandable and honest disagreement among well-intentioned leaders of both parties—and that is as it should be. In a two-party system there must be room for differences of opinion not only between parties but also within each party. The day we set up in the United States a different party for every group having different views, we will be well on our way down the dreary road some of our friends abroad with multiple party systems are traveling.

Within recent months it has repeatedly been said that a new brand of leadership is required for the space age.

The space age does present a tremendous challenge to the United States, the free world, and the part of the world that is not free. It is going to require leadership that is able to meet that challenge, and meet it effectively—leadership which is imaginative, leadership which does not concern itself so much with the past that it cannot prepare adequately for the problems and the challenges of the future.

Now if the implication intended by those who have raised this point is that we may not have that kind of leadership in the United States government today, I would like to make this comment: having sat as I have in the National Security Council throughout the past seven and a half years, and, of course, during the critical months when the new vista of outer space began to open for all of us, I feel confident that this Administration is aware of the challenge. It is prepared to take the necessary steps within the government to meet it.

His critics say that President Eisenhower has not been a strong leader, and yet they object to the leadership which ended the war in Korea, which handled the crisis in Suez, and which made two decisions to stand firm in the Formosa Straits —decisions which were controversial, in fact, partly because they were instances of strong leadership. His decision to go into Lebanon is another example of the President's strong leadership.

I would agree with Senator Kennedy, who has commented on this subject, that Lincoln was a strong leader and that Jackson was a strong leader. But I would disagree wholeheartedly with him that Eisenhower is not. Mr. Truman, in some respects, was a strong leader. His decision in Korea, his decision with regard to the use of the atomic bomb are two examples of strong, decisive leadership. But it cannot be said that one man is a strong leader because he pounds the table in order to get what he wants, while another is not a strong leader because he achieves his program through persuasion. Mr. Truman, for instance, was something of a table-pounder and he achieved some real results that way. President Eisenhower is a persuader and he, I submit, has gotten some real results, too.

In looking at Senator Kennedy's statement, I disagree with

his tendency to characterize leadership too much in terms of the personalities of the individual Presidents involved rather than in terms of what they accomplished.

An appraisal of leadership cannot be put down and described in terms of absolute, rigid, black-and-white categories. To say that one man is a strong leader and another man is a weak leader may be, on the basis of a whole record, a fair appraisal. But whether a man is a strong or a weak leader is determined by the results rather than the methods.

Now, looking to the '60s, I believe that the American people in their President are looking for a number of characteristics, whether he is a Democrat or a Republican. Among these are: first, that the President of the United States be a man who knows the great international and domestic issues. Certainly, I think most of the candidates on the Democratic side could qualify in this respect. They are students of the international and domestic scene. That knowledge, it seems to me, must then be combined with leadership qualities. The President must have the ability to gain support for the policies he believes are in the best interests of the nation.

When we speak of strong leadership, there is sometimes a tendency for people to say that what we need, whenever some kind of a crisis comes up, is for somebody to rush out and charge and lead the people in the proper direction up to the mountaintop. Now this is an understandable temptation. It is easy, when a difficult international issue comes up, to characterize those who may be opposing your policies as devils of the worst type and to engage in, shall I say, rash and impulsive language.

But in the '60s—in addition to knowledge of the issues, in addition to understanding of world affairs, in addition to the basic ability that any leader must have to gain support for his policies—the American people and the free world need in the American Presidency a man who has sound and sober judgment—a man who in a crisis will be cool, a man who won't go off half-cocked, a man who will resist the temptation (and the temptation will sometimes be great) to give the appearance of leadership when, actually, his speaking out rashly may set off a chain of circumstances that would be disastrous to the whole world. So I would urge that those who are examining this problem of leadership not be fooled by appearances, that they look beyond gestures and flamboyant speeches to what is actually accomplished. That is the lasting measure of true leadership.

Another criterion—perhaps an obvious one—is that a leader must, in fact, lead. It concerns me that apparently some people assume that the weight of the mail rather than the weight of the evidence should be the controlling factor in guiding those who determine American policy.

The expression of opinion by people to their elected representatives, by mail or otherwise, is constructive and helpful but it can never be considered the decisive factor in determining the course of policy.

If we indulge in the kind of thinking which assumes that important policy decisions should be made on the basis of opinion polls, we might as well decide now to surrender our position of world leadership to the Communists and to become a second-rate nation.

You cannot develop foreign policy or domestic policy for that matter on the basis of what random letters show the people will support in the light of the minimum and often misleading information available to them.

It is the responsibility of a leader to lead public opinion—not just to follow it. He must get all the facts before making a decision and then he must develop support for that decision among the people by making the facts known to them.

In a Presidential campaign, a problem often arises on the subject of personal abuse—or mudslinging, as it is called. As to whether this coming election campaign will be a mudslinging campaign, I can only say that it certainly will not be so far as I am concerned.

I believe the Presidential campaign should be a hard-hitting contest on the great issues before the American people. That is one of its purposes, to give the people a choice in the field of foreign and domestic policy where the candidates may disagree. Where a campaign is hard-hitting on the issues, it tends not to be a mudslinging campaign.

Many people have wondered, on this subject, whether religion would be an issue in this campaign. All of us agree, of course, that it should not be an issue. I can think of nothing that would be more damaging to the country. I can think of nothing that would be more personally repugnant to me than to raise what I call a personal issue like religion in a Presidential contest. My own view is that the country has moved pretty far along the way toward better understanding in the years since 1928, and I cannot believe that the so-called religious issue will have the impact in this campaign that it did in 1928.

I believe that a candidate should make no personal attacks, and that he should answer none. But I believe further that each candidate in a campaign has not only the right but the responsibility to attack the record of his opponent—his voting record, his speeches through the years, his basic ideas—if he disagrees with them. And his opponent, of course, has a right to defend them. That has been my policy in the past; it will continue to be in the future.

I would add that the most effective way of running for any office, assuming you want it, is to do a good job in the one you have. Beyond that, when a man is holding one position and has decided to run for another, he must get his views on the issues before the people.

We politicians, Republicans and Democrats both, owe it to our country and to the principles we stand for to put on nothing less than a fighting, hard-hitting campaign on the great issues confronting the nation. That is the kind of campaign we are going to have. I believe our opponents have the responsibility to criticize our record when they think we are wrong, and we have the responsibility to defend our record and to criticize theirs where we believe we are right. That is the only way, in an election campaign, that the people can make the right choice—through good, hard-hitting, sharp debate on the issues.

The overwhelming issue at the present time is the security and survival of the United States of America. That involves all the related issues: national defense, our foreign policy, and of course the nonmilitary aspects of the cold-war struggle.

When I speak of this as an issue, I do not mean that whoever may be the Democratic candidate or whoever may be the Republican candidate will disagree on all of its various facets. But I do mean that the American people, in judging which man they feel should be President of the United States in this critical period, will put as their first qualification whether or not the candidate is able to cope with this issue of survival in all of its aspects. They will consider who is best able from the standpoint of experience, and the policy that he may advocate during the course of the campaign, to offer constructive, creative leadership in this field.

As for the domestic issues, perhaps the most important will be the role of government in the economy of this country. Oversimplifying a very complex problem, the difference that I would see arising between the Republican and the Democratic candidate would be that the Republican candidate represent a philosophy that government should supplement rather than supplant individual and private enterprise. Not all, but most, of the potential Democratic candidates for the Presidency believe that government should take a larger role. They believe that the way to more economic growth is more government spending and more government activity than we presently have. If that is the issue it will be healthy for the country to debate and to get the verdict of the people as to which route they want to take. I have very strong views as to which route it should be.

I think that the reliance that we have placed on private enterprise and individual enterprise as the primary source of economic growth has been proven wise by our history. I think that this is where we ought to place our bets, looking toward this economic competition in the future.

Now, what should the Republican Party stand for in this campaign? We begin by saying that we are proud to run on the record of the present Administration, but we do not stop there. A record is something to build on—not something simply to stand on. And today, as I will indicate, "stand-pat, hold-the-line thinking" is not enough to meet the great challenges confronting the American people at home and abroad. The Republican Party has a great tradition of conservatism. We are not conservative because we are against progress; we are conservative because we are *for* progress. We are conservative because we know that the way to get better jobs, better schools, better health—all the progress that America wants—is through an application of conservative principles which brings out the best in people, rather than giving the entire responsibility over to a government in Washington, D.C. This is conservatism at its best.

2. *Strength for Peace and Freedom* [22]

There is no question but that the first consideration which must motivate any Administration is national survival. The United States must do what is necessary to maintain an adequate military posture: regardless of what any potential enemy of the United States may have, if that enemy should launch an attack, we must be able to retaliate and to destroy its war-making potential.

That is the principle that has guided this Administration in developing our current defense posture and in making crucial decisions for the future.

I realize that there are those who question this. Specialists in certain areas believe that we should put more emphasis on missiles, more on airborne alert, more on submarines, more on ground forces for limited war. I respect the right of any indi-

[22] The material in this section is derived from the following sources:

Remarks to the American Society of Newspaper Editors, Washington, D.C. April 18, 1959. Responses to questions at News Conference, Miami Beach, Florida. January 16, 1960. Responses to questions at the dinner program sponsored by the Businessmen's Advisory Committee of the School of Business Administration of Wayne State University, and the Wayne University Chapter of Alpha Kappa Psi, Detroit, Michigan. February 15, 1960. Televised Press Conference, Los Angeles Press Club, Los Angeles, California. February 18, 1958. Remarks at the National Brotherhood Award Dinner of the National Conference of Christians and Jews, Cleveland, Ohio. February 27, 1958. Remarks at the Sixty-sixth Annual Convention of the General Federation of Women's Clubs, Asheville, North Carolina. June 5, 1957. Responses to questions at the Conference with Representatives of the Four Armed Services, Washington, D.C. July 29, 1957. "The Greater Menace," Address presented at the Conference on University Contracts Abroad sponsored by the Committee on Institutional Projects Abroad of the American Council on Education, Denver, Colorado. November 14–15, 1957. Remarks at the Annual Meeting of the National Association of Manufacturers, New York, New York. December 6, 1957.

vidual to express his opinion on any aspect of the over-all decision. But I submit that the decision finally has to be made by someone who knows all the facts, who is experienced, who places the principle of security above any other consideration.

In view of the great and entirely legitimate debate that has been going on in regard to our military posture, let me say this: I have sat in the councils of this Administration; I have heard these matters debated; and in my mind there is no question but that, over-all—taking into consideration all of our weapons, personnel, and resources—the United States is stronger than any potential aggressor in the world.

I can say further that we have a program which we believe will maintain that strength in the future. Of course, in this age of rapid technological change, it is the responsibility of the United States constantly to reexamine its programs in the defense area and to make any changes that new facts may indicate are necessary—always to maintain such strength as will deter aggression and keep the peace.

How big a defense budget must the American people support to accomplish this objective? I realize that tax cuts and a reduction in the Federal budget would be most welcome. There is a time for such action. There is also a time for realism. And this is just such a time. The lowest taxes, the highest profits, the best wages in history will not make any difference if we are not around to enjoy them.

Militarily the United States and the free world today are stronger, over-all, than any potential aggressor. We have the will, ability, and resources to catch up in those areas where we may be behind and to retain our position of superiority.

We must spend whatever is necessary to accomplish this objective. This is not the same, however, as writing a blank check for unlimited defense spending. Our guard must be kept up for an indefinite period of tension. We must plan and budget for the long run.

While the strain on the Soviet economy will be greater than on ours, we must nevertheless make sure that ours can absorb the strain. We must continue to wage an unceasing battle against waste and duplication, not only in nonmilitary government activities but in the Defense Department as well. We need a hard defense, full of muscle, bare of fat.

There is no question but that *some* waste and duplication is inevitable. It could not be eliminated entirely in a department charged with the responsibility of spending the billions we allocate to national defense. But the occasional waste that is impossible to avoid is insignificant compared with the almost limitless waste and destruction of a nuclear war. If we are to make an error in this field, let us make it on the side of having too much defense rather than too little.

As for the willingness of the American people to support the burden of national defense over a long period of time, I feel sure that they will support as big a defense budget as they believe they need to. If the American people know the facts of a situation, they will meet their responsibilities. It is the task of those of us in positions of leadership, therefore, to lay before the people the great stakes in the world today—to point out to them that when we appropriate money for defense at home, when we appropriate money for foreign assistance to our allies and to the neutrals abroad, we do so because the alternatives are either defeat, or surrender without war. And this, I know, no American citizen will tolerate. If he realizes what the danger is and knows, too, that by continuing to support the necessary appropriations we can eventually reach a position where we can have our independence assured and have it assured without war—the American citizen will support the necessary appropriations.

I would qualify what I have just said by indicating only that every well has a bottom, that there is an inevitable limit to what we can do. But within the limits of our resources, the

American people will meet their responsibilities. Of this I am utterly convinced.

If all this is true, some are asking, why then are we behind in our space program?

On a completely nonpolitical basis, I would say that the reason we are behind in developing the very large-size rockets which are needed to put large payloads in outer space is that we did little to begin our ballistic missile program until the mid-'50s, whereas the Russians began to make an all-out effort in this particular area in 1946 and 1947. The failure of the previous Administration to launch a full-scale program in time was not essentially political but was chiefly military in character. At the time the Russians started their program, we relied on the tremendous striking force of our heavy bombers, which we had in great numbers. Warhead size in those days was so large, furthermore, that we did not believe it worthwhile to develop the huge missiles necessary to replace the bomber. The Soviets, however, did, and concentrated on them at that time. So much for why we are behind in this one area of rocketry and why we are now going all-out to catch up and capture the lead.

Certainly we should never underestimate our opponents, but it is also dangerous to overestimate them and underestimate ourselves: this might create a false impression in their minds as to our weakness and their strength. If the Soviet leaders actually believe there is a gap between their total military strength and ours, this belief could lead to disastrous miscalculation. Moreover, if there were such a gap—an over-all military gap as distinguished from a gap in one specialized area—it would definitely weaken our position vis-à-vis the Soviet Union at the bargaining table.

However, at present there is no such gap: the United States and the free world today have military strength which is great enough to meet and defeat any aggressor, if aggression is launched against the free world.

Looking to the immediate future, what the "missile gap" refers to is the claim that three or four years from now, if the intelligence estimates we have on the Soviet Union are accurate, they will have more intercontinental ballistic missiles than we have. Our answer is that, while that specific situation may arise, the time will never come when our over-all strength will not be sufficient so that the Communists could not risk an attack on us without suffering damage in return that they would not be willing to bring upon themselves.

We know we have this strength. And I think the Soviet leaders know it, too. As long as we retain it, when our negotiators go to international conferences and when the President goes to a summit conference, they can deal from a position of strength.

And, if the determination of the American people continues as I know it will, and if our allies continue to take the strong stand that they are taking with us now, I see no time in the foreseeable future when the free world will be in such a position that the Soviet Union will be able either to beat or blackmail us into submission.

Having said as much, let me add this: it is important that our outer-space development be under the control of a civilian agency. The potentials of outer space are so vast, so nearly limitless, that we must make positive plans to probe this potential in all its aspects.

One of the serious problems of our military-scientific relationship is the perhaps understandable reluctance of military people to free science for the investigation of areas in which the end result has no particular military application.

Control of space development by a military agency would mean that peaceful exploration of space would assume a minor role. But it is essential that the military and the peaceful uses of space be explored with equal intensity.

In this whole field of outer space, I do not believe we could make a greater mistake than to limit what we do to military needs and military thinking. If we did, our scientists would be limited in their research, in effect, to what our military men consider is possible and useful. We must give our scientists in the fields of basic research, and applied research also, the funds necessary to enable them to explore the unknown just for the sake of exploring it. Only in such a way will we find out what real significance it may have.

The significance of outer-space exploration for peaceful purposes may be tremendous. As Dr. Teller has pointed out on several occasions, it may be possible to find a method of controlling weather through the experiments that we are making in outer space. As he told me once in my office, no one can tell you that we *can* control the weather, but, on the other hand, no scientist will tell you that we cannot. We must support a research program which has vision enough to allow us to find out.

I might mention in this connection another very important issue: in this whole area of scientific development, one of our greatest assets is that we have allies whose scientists are very able, and with whom we can and should cooperate. Instead of simply duplicating what scientists in England, Germany, France, and other allied countries are doing, we should complement their work. Such cooperation can have tremendous possibilities. We need legislation from the Congress to enable that cooperation to be as effective as it should be, and I am hopeful that Congress will take the action necessary.

Sometimes there is a tendency for us in the United States to go to extremes in our reactions to events—as we did when the first Soviet satellite went into orbit. We are a very volatile people. We can be very high one day and very low the next. We have newly come—very newly, as a matter of fact—to a position of power in world affairs. Last year we marked but the hundredth anniversary of Theodore Roosevelt's birth, and it was only under his Presidency that the United States became, in a real sense, a world power. What we need, of course, is a mature reaction to the ups and downs that we are going to have—inevitably—in world affairs. We are not always going to be first in every field. We are going to suffer occasional reverses internationally.

The mission of the United States, as I see it, is essentially very simple. We want for others what we have for ourselves: independence for our nation, freedom for our people, and equality on the face of the earth. If we are going to fulfill that mission, we need inspired leadership not only in Washington but throughout this land. We need not only a sense of urgency in times of crises but a sense of maturity which will enable us to take our defeats and our setbacks, learn from them, and then go on to greater accomplishments in the future.

3. *A Dynamic Economy for America* [23]

In the critical years that face us, years in which the destiny of the world will be shaped for decades to come, I believe our success or failure will be determined in the realm of ideas. If this is to be the critical area of decision, it is essential that we constantly reexamine our ideas—the principles that motivate our actions—to see if they can actually prevail.

[23] The material in this section is derived from the following sources: "A Blueprint for America's Future," Address before the Fiftieth Anniversary Conference, Harvard Business School, Boston, Massachusetts. September 6, 1958. Remarks at Chicago "Dinner with Ike," Chicago, Illinois. January 27, 1960. Television appearance before the Los Angeles Press Club, Los Angeles, California. February 17, 1959. Remarks to American Society of Newspaper Editors, Washington, D.C. April 18, 1959. Responses to questions at the dinner program sponsored by the

If we are to judge the worth of our American ideas solely in terms of results, we can point to a record of cultural and economic progress unsurpassed in world history.

In the past fifty years our gross national product has quadrupled. Translating this dramatic figure into individual terms, we find that during this same period per capita income has increased from $188 to $2,032 a year, the number of homeowners has gone from 7 to 30 million, the annual production of automobiles has increased from 4,000 to as many as 7 million, the number of refrigerators in use from 23,000 to 47 million.

During the same fifty-year period, primary and secondary-school attendance has increased from 7 to 40 million, child labor has been substantially abolished, and 86 per cent of our labor force has been covered by social security.

We have not yet reached the goal Theodore Roosevelt proclaimed in his Square Deal speech at Osawatomie, Kansas, fifty years ago—that of giving every American an equal place at the starting line—but we have made more progress toward that objective than anyone dreamed was possible.

I recognize that among many of the critics of our much maligned "affluent society" it has become something of a fashion to deplore and condemn the mere conveniences of living as signs of our excessive materialism, as though these necessarily precluded the successful achievement of our real and proper aim—the full realization of the physical, mental, and spiritual capacity of every individual.

Self-examination of this character is healthy and constructive

---

Businessmen's Advisory Committee of the School of Business Administration of Wayne State University and the Wayne University Chapter of Alpha Kappa Psi, Detroit, Michigan. February 15, 1960. Remarks at the Salute to Republicans Dinner, New York, New York. January 20, 1958. Remarks at the Annual Dinner of the Bureau of Advertising, American Newspaper Publishers' Association, New York, New York. April 24, 1958. Remarks at the Sixty-fifth Annual Meeting of the Iron and Steel Institute, New York, New York. May 23, 1957.

in a free society, but I respectfully submit that few Americans are interested in material things as ends in themselves. We know that material well-being and spiritual and cultural achievement are related. It is as true today as when the Roman poet said it 2,000 years ago that man must first eat before he can become a philosopher.

It is tremendously important today that the United States sustain to the ultimate degree possible a high rate of economic growth. Particularly in view of the world situation, with the Soviet Union moving ahead vigorously on the economic front, it is essential that we produce at the highest possible rate.

Every time the American economy suffers even a slight shock there are reverberations in the economies of free nations throughout the world. A major or prolonged downturn in the United States would have catastrophic effects not only on our own country but on our friends abroad. The greatest gainers from such an event would be Mr. Khrushchev and his cohorts in the Kremlin.

However, we could make no more stupid blunder than to rest our case on materialism alone. This is all that our opponents have to offer. We have much more.

Throughout all our history, America's leaders have recognized that the principles on which the United States was founded—freedom, equality, and constitutionalism—have universal validity and applicability. The rights we have defended are natural rights which come from God. All men, we truly believe, are created equal. In this sense, America indeed has a mission: a destiny to defend, preserve, and extend the rights of man. If America makes this clear we cannot fail to receive the support of most of the people of the world.

What then is the major reason for the Communist appeal in the world today? Its appeal is not in the Marxist philosophy as such. Communism with all its evils has appeal primarily because it appears to be on the march—advocating and promising change.

Our answer, therefore, must be to talk less of the threat of the Communist revolution and more of the promise of the American Revolution. This is what the world wants to hear. We have nothing to fear provided we remain true to the best elements in our tradition.

We must make known throughout the world the exciting fact that the American Revolution, which captured the imagination of the world 180 years ago, did not end at Yorktown. It is a living, vital idea today; it is the idea which we believe can most surely satisfy the aspirations of people the world over for economic progress, individual freedom, and national independence.

The solution to the problem we face is not to be found simply in better information and propaganda. In the words of Hegel, "Nations are what their deeds are." And a nation is strong only when it is engaged in realizing great objectives. Once it loses its sense of mission, a nation's days are numbered.

I suggest that we examine the American idea in the light of these considerations to see if it has the vitality and drive to prevail. What are the dangers we must guard against and the goals we should seek to attain?

Let us recognize at the outset that we shall not win this competition with communism simply by standing still. We are ahead now, but the only way to stay there is to move still further ahead. Let it not be said of our generation that we set as our goal simply holding our own. Let us resist the temptation to be satisfied by merely putting another guard on the cash box. Let us, on the contrary, boldly expand the heritage we have been so fortunate to receive—expand it to new heights both materially and spiritually.

Stand-pat, defensive thinking is not adequate for the challenge we face either at home or abroad.

Those of us who are economic conservatives (and I would put myself in that category) regard our conservatism as essentially and truly progressive. We oppose nonconservative policies—those policies which look to government for the solution of all problems, those policies which are not based on fiscal responsibility—but we oppose them not because their goals for better housing and better standards of living are too high, but because they are actually too low. We oppose them because such programs will not work.

The reason we are conservative is that history tells us this is the way to real, sustained progress. If we continue to be conservative, if we continue to have faith in the private-enterprise system in this country, if we continue to supplement that system only where private enterprise cannot or will not do the job—supplement it then with government action—this is the way to progress. Indeed, this is the kind of conservatism I believe in.

A quote from Tolstoy is very appropriate at this point. It seems to me to spotlight the weakness of the position of those who say government should control the economy in order to serve the people. It goes something like this:

"I sit on a man's back choking him and making him carry me, and yet assure myself and others that I am very sorry for him and wish to ease his lot by all possible means—except by getting off his back."

That is exactly the position the government is in when it does too much. All of our government policies must be designed merely to encourage and stimulate individual Americans to make their maximum contributions to the realization of the nation's potential.

Without apology, we conservatives believe that private enterprise is generally more efficient and more desirable than government enterprise, and that it is the major force for growth and prosperity in our economy. We believe that social progress can best be achieved by government action which supplements rather than supplants what private enterprise can do.

We have unshakable faith that the way to achieve our goals

is by the free choices of millions of individual consumers, by the productive efforts of free management and labor, and by local and state action wherever possible.

The record proves that our faith in freedom is well placed. Economic policies based on encouraging free enterprise get results—they work.

As long as they are left free of arbitrary controls, the American people will continue to achieve greater and greater abundance, with fair shares for everyone.

To be sure, government must play a part in achieving our goals.

1. Our tax system must be revised so that it will encourage rather than curb new initiative, ingenuity and enterprise.

2. Small business must be encouraged and stimulated so that it can continue its invaluable service of pumping new blood and new ideas into our free-enterprise system.

3. We must recognize and develop the full potential of millions of our fellow citizens who are now denied adequate opportunity for education and employment because of their race or color.

4. We must develop a new program for agriculture rather than adopting the unworkable political approach of freezing America's farmers in an obsolete, rigid system which can only lead to a dreary cycle of surpluses, controls, and depressed farm income.

5. We must have vision to develop an enlightened and far-reaching program for foreign trade if we are to have adequate markets for the increasing production of our growing economy.

Let us look at three specific areas in which government must play a part if we are to push forward with the vigor and boldness the times require.

1. A dynamic and growing economy is bound to cause hardships to some of the people involved in the process of change.

As new businesses come into being and others grow, some will be replaced. And in a free economy we must expect readjustments from time to time—which, in turn, will mean temporary unemployment for some American workers.

With these facts in mind, consideration should be given to instituting permanent reforms in our system of unemployment insurance.

a. Specifically, to the extent feasible, the 12 million workers not now covered should be brought under our unemployment compensation system.

b. The prolongation of benefit periods put in effect in 1958 as a temporary measure should be made permanent.[24]

c. The Federal and state governments should work together toward the objective of establishing higher minimum standards for the level of benefits, their duration, and their coverage.

These proposals are sound not only for reasons of plain humanity, but also because the flow of income provided by more adequate unemployment compensation serves to cushion the impact of the business cycle. The faster we carry out this basic reform, the greater can be our assurance that occasional setbacks in economic activity, such as are bound to occur in a free economy, will remain brief and mild.

2. A second major economic problem is inflation. In order to maintain high production, in order to have real economic growth, more jobs, and higher standards of living, it is necessary to have a sound fiscal base. And to have a sound base,

---

[24] In 1958, as an "emergency" measure, Federal funds were made available to the states for supplementary unemployment payments for those who had used up their state benefits—up to 26 additional weeks at no more than 50 per cent of the amount of regular state payments. A permanent program along these lines would probably have the effect of setting national minima with respect to duration and amount of unemployment compensation payments, with primary responsibility left to the states, however, and with room for local variation above the "floor" thus established.

we must have reasonable price stability. Unchecked inflation prevents the planning for the future by business and other private investors which is essential for economic growth.

We often hear it said that the only people who care about a sound dollar are the bankers and the stockbrokers and the rich. The truth is that they are the very people who need be least concerned about inflation, because they can hedge against it. The people who should be most concerned are the people who have fixed incomes, the people who work in our factories, the people who invest their hard-earned dollars for their old age, for unemployment, for a rainy day—and then find that when they cash in their insurance and pensions, they are not worth as much as the original labor involved.

To use a personal example: when I was growing up, my mother and father saved their money through the years to buy a life insurance policy. It was a relatively small one by modern standards—$3,000 in the New York Life.

I remember year after year, when those premiums came around, particularly during the late '20s and '30s, how difficult it was to meet them. And the money that they invested in that policy, which my mother received when my father died four years ago, was worth but a third of the effort that he put in when he earned it.

I think this is wrong, and I think that no administration should allow this to happen if it can possibly be avoided.

Inflation robs the aged of their savings.

It is an automatic pay cut for those on fixed salaries.

It is a tax on life insurance policies.

It leads ultimately to consumer resistance and rebellion.

It would be a mistake to try to stimulate economic activity without also trying to curb inflation. Otherwise, in whatever action we take, we are simply buying trouble later on.

When we look into the causes of inflation we find three main areas that must be watched closely—the monetary and fiscal policies of government, the cost and price policies of business, and the impact of wage demands upon costs and prices.

A deficit running into billions of dollars in the Federal budget is a major inflationary factor. We must learn that we cannot add new programs to the Federal budget unless we are prepared to levy the taxes to pay for them, on substantially a pay-as-you-go basis.

I completely reject the fiscal philosophy of those who suggest that as the national income increases, the expenditures of the Federal government should increase in proportion. It is true that to the extent that a larger population requires larger expenditures for certain government services, the budget will necessarily increase. But it is sheer nonsense to suggest that government should always take as much out of the national economy as the economy can stand. We should spend for government only what we need to spend—even if this may be less than we are able to spend.

Inflationary pressures are also created by the excessive use of private credit. We must follow credit policies which will limit and control these inflationary excesses.

However, it is completely unrealistic to assume that inflation can be controlled entirely by the monetary policies of the Federal Reserve System or the spending policies of the Federal government.

Recognizing as we do that government has its part to play, we must never forget one fundamental principle: what distinguishes the American idea from the Communist is that we believe the surest source of economic productivity and national progress is private rather than government enterprise.

Business as well as government has a job to do in preventing inflation. It must redouble its efforts to cut down on waste and to find real economies in production and distribution. Above all, it must have the daring and imagination to price for volume sales with low unit profits.

Organized labor also has a major responsibility in this area.

During the postwar years labor sought and received large wage increases in order to keep up with inflation. The momentum of this process continued even during the years when the consumer price level remained stable. The result was an upward push of costs and prices that was an important factor, for example, in the inflationary trend starting in late 1955.

America's labor leaders must exercise restraint in this connection. The labor leader has a responsibility to fight for the best interests of labor union members. Obviously union members would like to have higher wages, but they also want jobs. When higher costs price their product out of the market, they are out of a job. Wage increases which are not based on increased productivity mean higher prices, lower sales, and fewer jobs for union members. A round of this type of wage increases can have a depressing effect on the entire economy.

The remedy for this evil most consistent with our free institutions is self-discipline at the bargaining table. Unless this remedy is used, the pressure from consumers for government action to control inflation will become irresistible. Likewise there will be strong demands to control by law those union activities that are monopolistic in character. This can be avoided if our union leaders in their contract negotiations are guided by this basic principle—that wage increases which force price increases are not in the best interests of union members themselves.

This position is in no sense anti-union. On the contrary, what we want is a return to the wage policies that have been traditional in the American labor movement. The pattern of spectacular competitive wage increases, leading inevitably to higher prices, is relatively new in American labor. It is time to return now to the healthier, sounder approach which made American labor the greatest free trade union movement in the world.

3. Our third major economic problem is that of tax reform.

In light of the enormous expenditures required of the Federal government at the present time, this would appear to be a completely academic question. But we are faced here with a dilemma.

There should be concern about the size of the Federal budget. If we were to have a debt that continued to go up and up and up, the inevitable result would be a vicious circle: the amount we would have to pay for interest, for example, would be so unconscionably high that the amount we could allocate to services, to national defense, and the like, would be proportionately less and less than it should be.

I believe that the United States should spend all that is necessary. But it is the responsibility of a national Administration not to spend one cent more, and not to allow the debt to rise if that can be avoided.

Yet, if we wait for needed tax reform until we believe we can afford a tax cut, our economy will have been denied vitally needed stimuli for growth.

The importance of economic growth to our fiscal position is indicated by the fact that if our economy were to grow at the rate of 5 per cent a year we would have $10 billion more in tax receipts in 1962 than if we were to continue to grow at the recent rate of about 2 per cent.

Consequently, I suggest we give thought to the following proposals:

In these days of rapid technological change we need more liberal treatment of depreciation for business taxation purposes. Only in this way can we stimulate "risk" investment in new plants and equipment.

We should consider the economic effects of downward adjustments in business taxes. There are strong reasons to believe that the stimulating effects of even a small cut in the corporate tax rate of 52 per cent would lead to more rather than less revenue.

Consideration should also be given to a complete over-hauling of the present hodgepodge of excise taxes. If just the taxes on liquor and cigarettes were left as they are and all other excise taxes were abolished, a general manufacturers' excise tax of approximately 1½ per cent could be substituted and would bring in as much revenue as is presently obtained.

In the area of personal income, the almost confiscatory rates in the highest brackets stifle and prevent risk-taking and en-courage devices for tax-avoidance. The small loss of revenue caused by some reduction of these rates would inevitably be offset by new investment and business expansion.

I realize that for someone in political life even to suggest consideration of such proposals as these must seem somewhat foolhardy. The charge will inevitably be made that such re-forms will benefit business and not the people. I suppose this would be a good place for a politician to plead the Fifth Amendment, but I am going to take the more risky course of pleading guilty—but not as charged.

Let us understand once and for all that "business" *is* the "people." The people own it. And their ownership is becoming ever more widely diffused. They make their living out of business. They depend on business for progress, for oppor-tunity, for their mutual well-being, and for the development and production of the military equipment which shields the nation against aggression.

Prosperity for the American people is inseparable from prosperity for American business. We cannot raise the floor of security unless we first raise the ceiling of opportunity. The best way for the American people to improve their living standards is through policies that promote maximum business growth.

In summary, then, we must not allow our legitimate concern over the Federal budget to put us in a strait jacket which will keep us from doing what we ought to do to ensure economic growth. Our goal should be to fashion a tax structure which will create more jobs, more income, and more genuine security.

These remarks should not be concluded without a brief outline of some of the new frontiers for America in the years ahead. The exciting potentials of a dynamic, growing American economy are almost unbelievable.

A $750 billion gross national product is within our reach by 1975 if we grow at an annual rate of 3 per cent—and by 1968, if we can increase our growth rate to 5 per cent.

Completion of our 41,000-mile interstate highway system; doubling the facilities of our colleges and universities; elimination of the pockets of poverty that trouble the conscience of a rich nation; restoring the vitality and beauty of our cities through urban renewal—all these goals are attainable well within this generation.

And when we consider the explosive progress which will result from expanded research in industry, medicine, and other areas, the prospects are breathtaking in their magnitude.

But exciting as these prospects are, the greatest goal of all lies in the international area. Arnold Toynbee wrote in 1951 that 300 years from now this bloody twentieth century may well be remembered not for its splitting of the atom, nor for its diminutions of distance and disease, nor even for its shattering wars. Rather, it will go down in history as "having been the first age since the dawn of civilization in which people dared to think it practicable to make the benefits of civilization available to the whole human race." This is the ultimate challenge for us in this last half of the twentieth century.

If our statesmen and businessmen can keep pace with the break-throughs of our scientists, the last half of the twentieth century will see us approach realization of this objective. The critical question is—will this progress be achieved in a climate of freedom or in a climate of slavery?

No people could have a greater mission than to play a

part in seeing to it that the decision is made on the side of freedom. It is not enough to say that this responsibility rests with our statesmen and diplomats alone. It is not enough to increase, as we should, our pitifully inadequate appropriations for developmental loans, technical assistance, and information. To win this worldwide struggle, our national effort—just like the Communist effort—must be total.

4. *The Challenge to American Education* [25]

We hear a great deal these days about the challenge presented to the United States by the Soviet space program. The military and economic strength which this program demonstrates have understandably been of primary concern to us.

But without question the fundamental challenge lies in the

[25] The material in this section is derived from the following sources:

"Price Stability and Economic Growth," Address to the Economic Conference, Washington, D.C. November 2, 1959. Responses to questions at the program of the Detroit Committee for the Seven Eastern Women's Colleges, Inc., Detroit, Michigan. February 15, 1960. Responses to questions at the dinner program sponsored by the Businessmen's Advisory Committee of the School of Business Administration of Wayne State University, and the Wayne University Chapter of Alpha Kappa Psi, Detroit, Michigan. February 15, 1960. Responses at News Conference, Detroit, Michigan. February 15, 1960. Remarks before the Thirty-fifth Annual Meeting of American Football Coaches Association, Philadelphia, Pennsylvania. January 8, 1958. Remarks at the All-Congress Dinner of the 1958 National Nuclear Energy Congress, Chicago, Illinois. March 19, 1958. Remarks on NBC Television Program observing Chemical Progress Week, Washington, D.C. April 9, 1957. Remarks at the Business and Industry Luncheon, De Pauw University, Greencastle, Indiana. May 11, 1957. Remarks at the Centennial Convention of the National Education Association, Philadelphia, Pennsylvania. July 3, 1957. Remarks at the Fifteenth Annual Meeting of the Board of Trustees of the Committee for Economic Development, Washington, D.C. November 21, 1957. Remarks at the Twenty-ninth Anniversary Dinner of Yeshiva University, New York, New York. December 15, 1957.

field of education. That is why the American educational system is being subjected today to one of the most penetrating periods of criticism in our national history.

However, as we consider the deficiencies of American education we should not lose sight of its strong points. Today the United States leads the world in the breadth of its public education.

Only four other countries—Norway, Sweden, the Netherlands, and Japan—share with us the accomplishment of having 99 per cent of their elementary-school-age children attending school.

The percentage of students beyond elementary-school age who actually attend high school and college is higher in America than in any other country.

We have more classrooms and other equipment for our student population than any other nation.

As a result, we have more technically and professionally trained people in our population than any other nation, and we have reduced illiteracy to 3 per cent of the total population —an accomplishment exceeded only by Norway and Sweden.

Our educational system has many admirable qualitative features. We are striving to prepare our students to be participating citizens in a great democracy. In our classrooms today, students discuss the real problems of our time. They visit farms and factories, to see for themselves the bases of economic life. They have a large measure of self-government, again a preparation for good citizenship in the future.

But for all our present well-being, for all our accomplishments, many serious problems remain to be solved. And some are so serious that they threaten the survival of much that we hold dear.

I think that today we would find a considerable amount of nationwide support for these propositions: (1) in some segments of American education we need more discipline; (2) in some schools and colleges we need a greater competitive spirit than we have had in recent years, particularly with regard to grades and academic standards; and (3) we need more emphasis on the training of scientists and engineers, in view of our deficiency in this respect vis-à-vis the Soviet Union and in view of the challenge which the Soviet Union presents for the future.

We also need more scientific education for the general public. If our national scientific activity is to be maintained at an adequate level, the American people will have to have deeper motivations than a desire for immediate practical benefits, however important these may be. The new age will require of the public generally a high degree of scientific literacy and the blending of science into our total culture and way of life.

Increasingly, major national decisions involve scientific and technological decisions. Obtaining adequate support for projects that have obvious military value is relatively easy. But we need a high level of public understanding to develop sound national policies with respect to long-term space science and exploration programs.

We also need such understanding to provide continued support for the instruments, institutions, and attitudes which will ensure sound scientific progress. It is not that we want to make all of our citizens into scientists: what we must try to do is to provide for the nonscientists the insight and understanding with respect to science which we have historically sought to give to all of our citizens in the field of the humanities.

However, it would be a mistake in reacting to the Soviet challenge to swing to such an extreme that we might lose our present advantages. We do not want an unbalanced, warped society which would be the inevitable result if undue emphasis were placed on scientific materialism. We want to develop the whole man, not merely one phase of the intellect. We want all our students to be well-rounded and responsible future parents and citizens.

We do not want to ape the Russians and eventually become simply a pale carbon copy of the scientific materialists who run the Soviet Union. It is well and altogether proper that the primary emphasis in any government program should be in the scientific and military field. But we should not make this emphasis so great that we lose a proper balance in the development of those who will be our government officials, those who will run our businesses, those who will be our teachers and scholars, those in the field of social science and the arts.

In our understandable desire not to fall behind in technical fields, let us continue in our educational process to place proper emphasis on the humanities and on the responsibilities that we have as citizens.

The men and women coming from our colleges and universities must be more than simply scientific and technical automatons. They must be people who can assume the responsibilities of citizenship in a free society.

This, I find, is a view which is held not only by educators, but also by many of our top scientists. They well recognize that we must have more highly trained scientists and engineers if we are to maintain our position of world leadership. But we must not and will not have them by forced draft or arbitrary and artificial selection. The scientists and engineers who have contributed so much to America's greatness chose their careers freely. They realized the importance of this work; they were challenged by its vast frontiers; they saw its opportunities and were willing to undergo the rigorous preparation. They made their choice with greater freedom than is allowed anywhere else in the world. This is the important ingredient of America's scientific and technical greatness, and so it must continue to be.

Too often we hear the superficial and pat formula that the answer to all of our problems in the educational field is more classrooms, more teachers, more scholarships, and more scientists. Action on these fronts is of course essential. But we shall miss the target completely if we do not recognize at the outset that our major problem is quality and not mere quantity of education.

To illustrate: perhaps the most fundamental weakness in many of our schools is that students are not allowed to face the challenge of failure. Passing is becoming automatic. Efforts are made to judge the child and his efforts, not his achievements. Many educators acknowledge these shortcomings, but state that this is the democratic approach.

They say it is more important to help students to adjust to one another and to feel the warmth of success than it is to demand rigorous achievement. I sympathize with the humanitarian aims of these educators. But I submit that their approach does not measure up to the reality of life. When students leave school, they will find that success is far from automatic. Knowledge and achievement will count—not just good intentions. In the hard competition of life, they will have to face failure at some time or other. And since life is this way, our schools do not realistically prepare students if they ignore such realities.

It is good to have democracy in our educational system, but it is also necessary to have backbone, standards, and guidance. Young people want and need firm guidance. They may rebel against specific commands, but even the brashest of them knows that he has not the experience and wisdom to face the world unaided. As most parents have learned through experience, true parental love is firm, not indulgent.

We must recognize also that what and how our students are taught is as important as by whom and where. In this context, let us examine two other major criticisms which are currently being levelled at our school system.

There are too many soft subjects in the average curriculum, and not enough tough, challenging disciplines that develop the mind. We know that a soft physical life leads to flabby muscles and poor health. Similarly, a mental regime that lacks challenge leads to an underdeveloped brain and a weak intellect.

A related complaint is that too often we do not sufficiently challenge our superior students. Even when they are taking demanding subjects, they find that the level of teaching is geared to the least gifted student. Too many superior students are being lost among the normal and mediocre. We need to seek them out, to inspire them, to encourage the development of the intellectual disciplines that alone can make them attain their full potential and ultimately contribute their maximum to society.

It is estimated that our college population will be twice as large ten years from now as it is today. To meet this demand, we will need new physical facilities and more teachers.

The task of obtaining and keeping good teachers in our schools, colleges, and universities is becoming increasingly difficult. A dedicated teacher does not expect to earn as much in his chosen profession as he would in another field requiring similar qualifications. But he must have—and he is surely entitled to—compensation which will enable him to maintain the standards which his position requires.

For example, the average salary of all teachers in private colleges and universities in the United States in 1958 was only $4,700 a year. We can see how inadequate this is when we compare it with the $5,500 which was at the same time the average pay for all industrial workers in the city of Flint, Michigan. Unless steps are taken to remedy this situation, we can only expect that both the quality and number of those who choose teaching as a profession will decline.

But to have better schools, we must not only prevent any deterioration in the quality of our teachers, we must strive toward ever higher quality. As President Pusey of Harvard said a few years ago: "Classrooms in which there are teachers with no exceptional gifts are places merely to keep young people, not to educate them." We must give the best training we possibly can to those who mold the minds of our youth. We must develop teaching scholars, not teaching technicians. But most important, we must give teachers the salary, prestige, and backing that will attract the best minds to this honored profession.

There is, indeed, no more important problem in American education today than raising the compensation for our teachers, and according them the recognition they deserve.

This is a vital need, and certainly all over the country at all levels of education it is one that our local communities, our state legislatures, and our school boards must face up to.

How can we improve our educational system? We hear a great deal about what the Federal government can and should do. There are some who ask: why can't we have far greater Federal responsibility for education at the primary level, the secondary level, and the college level as well?

In the Soviet Union this would be the logical and only approach. But one of the matchless strengths of this nation is that our schools have always been primarily a local concern. The individual citizen is responsible, with his neighbor, for the quality and caliber of our total educational system.

One very important principle for us to bear in mind is that the hallmark of freedom is diversity. We do not want our educational standards established either in Washington or, for that matter, in the state capital, and made absolutely uniform for all of the people and all of the students in all of the schools.

There is a need for coordination. There is a need for leadership. But we must recognize that diversity in education, as in every other field, is one of the guarantees of freedom. The very fact that our colleges differ so greatly in their curricula and in their approach is one of the guarantees of freedom.

I believe very strongly that one of the great strengths of a free society is local control of the educational process. The closer we can keep the control and operation of our school system to the people, the more chance we have to avoid the development of a centralized all-powerful bureaucracy and remote control of something as important as what is taught the new generation of Americans.

Our task in the case of Federal aid to education is to reconcile these two problems: first, teachers should be paid more; but second, we want continued local control rather than Federal control. There are some who believe, perhaps with justification, that Federal contributions to teachers' salaries would promote bureaucratic centralization and ultimately Federal control.

The way to a reconciliation, in my view, is for the Federal government to limit its aid to school construction.[26] Where construction is involved, there is no suggestion of inhibiting control whatever.

Moreover, the Administration's program of Federal aid for school construction would have two beneficial effects on the position of our teachers. In this plan, recognition is given to those districts that make an extra effort with respect to teachers' salaries. In addition, if Federal grants are available for construction, local resources can be diverted from construction to teachers' pay—so indirectly, teachers will benefit. This kind of aid would thus enable schools, colleges, and universities to take better care of the teacher—and to provide more help for the students through scholarships and loans. I believe that this

[26] The core of the Administration-sponsored aid-to-education bills before the 86th Congress is a long-term program of matching grants (half-federal, half-state) to assist the states in servicing both interest charges and principal payments on school-construction bonds—three billion dollars worth of such bonds in the first five years. An annual federal outlay of some 85 millions is projected and, over a 30-year period, a total of up to 2.2 billions of dollars. This program would cover only construction projects—not salaries or other educational expenses. A special formula would favor those states making the greatest relative effort to meet their educational needs out of their own resources (i.e., the ratio of educational outlays to total state expenditures and total state income).

is not only an effective program but the one approach to this problem that satisfies both our most pressing needs and our insistence on local control.

Now let me add one further word with regard to the support of our public schools. I often meet in Washington with influential citizens who say: we are unalterably against Federal aid to education—period. They are honest in this opposition. They are against the school construction provisions which I favor because they think even that much Federal aid might result in Federal control. They say this is purely and exclusively a local responsibility. And then some of these same people go back home and vote against bond issues that would build a school or provide necessary funds for teachers' salaries. That is the kind of completely irresponsible activity that has to be vigorously opposed.

If we are going to have local control, we must have local responsibility. And this means that the local people have to assume it. Local people must look to the scale of salaries for their teachers; they must look to the adequacy of the schoolrooms; they must look to the standards which are maintained in their schools—and then do what is necessary to maintain or raise them.

An analogous problem is providing the necessary support for private colleges and universities. This, too, is becoming increasingly difficult.

The answer is not simply to expand tax-supported colleges and universities. Since 42 per cent of all our college graduates come from private schools, it is obvious that we need both types of institutions to meet the total national need. It would be a tragedy of the first magnitude if tax-supported state schools were gradually to drive private institutions out of existence.

Both large state institutions and smaller private colleges have their strong points. Perhaps the outstanding advantage offered by the small college is that the student can have intimate and personal contact with the teacher. In large institutions, classes—particularly in the crucially important first two years—are so large that class discussion is virtually impossible, and there is little personal relationship between teacher and student. In the small college, on the other hand, instruction is essentially individual and personal. The teacher has the opportunity to liberate and stimulate the student's mind so that he will be able to rise to the pinnacle of his creative ability. The teacher can encourage an attitude of mind and a desire to think which prepares the student to enter society with a desire to be of service. The small college can also offer a religious emphasis which is necessarily lacking in large state institutions.

As long as we have strong privately supported colleges and universities as well as state institutions, we will not run the risk of government domination and control which might develop if higher education were completely dependent on state and Federal government grants.

The problem of the small colleges will not be solved by enrolling more tuition-paying students. On the average, tuitions provide only half of the total cost of a college education. Nor is the answer to be found in raising tuitions. They are already so high that too many qualified students are unable to get a higher education. One recent survey disclosed that 40 per cent of the students in the top 5 per cent of their high-school classes did not go on to college. The United States cannot continue to afford this tragic waste of talent and ability.

Direct Federal aid to private colleges and universities is unlikely and, in many respects, undesirable, for such aid could impair the independent integrity which is the chief strength of the private institution.

Contributions from individuals are increasingly difficult to obtain because of high income tax rates. I believe that when the fiscal situation of the Federal government is such that we can afford a reduction in taxes, we should give the most serious

consideration to provisions which would encourage such contributions. And we should also consider various plans which
have been suggested for allowing tuitions and fees of both
public and private institutions to be treated as tax deductions.

A major new source of endowment income for private institutions must come from corporations and other business enterprises which compete today for the graduates the colleges are
producing. Such contributions should be considered just as
important an item of business expense as an investment in
basic research.

I hope that as a result of this great debate—about teachers'
salaries which are too low and about the quality and character
of education in general—there will develop a sharper sense of
responsibility on the part of businessmen, professional men,
and others in local communities throughout this country. It is
the citizens themselves who must take the initiative in raising
standards. American education will be no better and no worse
than the individual American wants it to be. Whether it takes
more classrooms, higher salaries, fewer frills, more algebra
and less square dancing, this responsibility cannot be passed
along to Washington. The burden is on all of us.

5. *Labor and the Steel Strike* [27]

We have all read and heard, these last two years, a good deal about labor racketeering. Much of the recent interest in this problem resulted from the investigations conducted during 1958 and 1959 by the McClellan Committee. This investigation served a useful purpose. It exposed the activities of union officials who broke faith with their own membership, and with the community at large. It also served to remind us that no leader of government, business, or labor is so big or so powerful that he cannot be made to account for his actions before the elected representatives of the people.

The question is: what legislation will best guard against such abuses in the future?

Most of these abuses have involved practices within certain unions which have not only violated the public interest but the interests of union members themselves. Thus the essential guideline to effective legislation must be to provide for more control by union members of their own unions. Union leaders must be responsible to union members, reporting on the conduct of the union's business and on the spending of union funds. Union members, in turn, must have control over their leaders through procedures which provide for free and fair

[27] The material in this section is derived from the following sources:
Remarks at the Sixtieth National Convention of the Veterans of Foreign Wars of the United States, Los Angeles, California. August 31, 1959. Responses to questions at television appearance before the Los Angeles Press Club, Los Angeles, California. February 17, 1959. "Price Stability and Economic Growth," Address to the Economic Conference, Washington, D.C. November 2, 1959. Letter to Alexander F. Jones of the Syracuse *Herald-Journal.* January 21, 1960. Responses to questions at News Conference, Detroit, Michigan. February 15, 1960. Remarks at the American Management Association Conference, New York, New York. May 20, 1958. Remarks at the Ninety-ninth Annual Commencement, Michigan State University, East Lansing, Michigan. June 9, 1957.

elections of officers—for what we call, in general, "union democracy." I think the Landrum-Griffin Bill does just this.[28]

Public opinion during the Committee hearings would probably have supported legislation so drastic that it would have curbed legitimate union activities as well as the abuses exposed in these hearings. But such severe legislation would have been unwise.

Organized labor today is going through a period of trial comparable to that endured by the business community some twenty years ago. Its leadership is being scrutinized and tested. The recent investigations showed that some union leaders have failed badly in their positions of trust.

But we should not repeat the mistake of twenty years ago and blame an entire movement for the blunders and crimes of a minority. Rather we should help outraged union members to restore honesty and integrity to their unions. The protection of the integrity of union welfare funds and the insurance of democratic procedures in the conduct of union business are the legitimate objectives of effective labor legislation. The aim of any legislation in this field must not be to weaken or destroy unions, but rather to give union members the tools they need to make all unions follow the sound practices which most of them follow today.

[28] The Labor-Management Reporting and Disclosure Act of 1959 (the so-called Landrum-Griffin Bill) which became law in September 1959 was an amalgam of various proposals—by the McClellan Committee, by the Administration, by Senators Kennedy and Ervin, and by Congressmen Landrum and Griffin—and contained, in essence, the major recommendations of the Administration in the following areas: (a) union member "bill of rights" with respect to frequent elections of union officers by secret ballot, information on the use of union funds, and limitations on nationally-controlled trusteeships of union locals; (b) tighter controls over secondary boycotts; (c) prohibition of organizational picketing; (d) provisions for regular reporting on union fiscal affairs, both to the Secretary of Labor and to the union membership; (e) barring of convicted criminals from union office; and (f) criminal penalties for failure to comply with the provisions of the Act.

This whole recent controversy provides a golden opportunity for American businessmen to encourage the honest and sincere men who constitute the great majority of union officers. Now is the time to build lasting good will in labor relations, rather than to ostracize all union leadership, good or bad, and create conditions which could only lead to bitter industrial strife in the years ahead.

Union democracy certainly provides the best solution to the problem of racketeering. But dishonesty in union leadership is not the only problem posed by the unions. The public needs protection from some extravagant practices that have arisen as the union movement has increased in power—such practices as are inevitable when any segment of our economy acquires too much power. For example, in the Administration-supported labor bill there were provisions to deal with and control secondary boycotts and to strengthen the Taft-Hartley Act in that respect, and also provisions to deal with what is called "blackmail" or "organizational picketing." These, too, are legitimate objects of effective labor legislation.

Antitrust legislation has often been suggested as a possible remedy for excessive union power, just as presently it is used to curb excessive power in corporations. I think this is an unrealistic proposal. The problem in the case of unions is very different from the problem in the case of corporations. Antitrust legislation applied to unions would not have the effect which those who favor it have in mind.

What is needed in the case of excessive union power is not a shotgun approach—and this is really the nature of antitrust laws—but an approach in which you aim carefully and selectively at specific abuses.

The Landrum-Griffin Bill, which has been much criticized by some sections of labor, took just such an approach. It struck at secondary boycotts, at jurisdictional strikes, and at internal labor practices in which union members were exploited by some unscrupulous leaders.

One major economic problem that faces us all today concerns the wage-price spiral, created to a large extent by wage increases which have not been based on productivity.

No one group in our economy should have a greater interest in controlling inflation than labor. This is particularly true today, for the wage contracts that are currently being negotiated have far more emphasis on fringe benefits than ever before. And the fringe benefits to which union members contribute month by month and year by year are going to be worth less and less, unless our fiscal policies protect the value of the dollar.

I personally believe that continuous study and selective Congressional action will be needed in the years ahead, in the interest of the long-term growth of our economy. We must seek to achieve a proper balance between labor and management— between big labor and big management as well as big labor and small management.

At present and in the years to come, we must steadfastly avoid adopting any legislation that would have the effect of weakening the trade union movement as such. It is our great good fortune to have a strong free trade union movement in the United States. One has only to travel to countries that do not have such an institution to realize how fortunate we are. We owe a great debt of gratitude to our union leaders for their firm position on the important issues of freedom versus slavery, political as well as economic. The American trade union movement has moved effectively in virtually all of its various segments against Communist infiltration and domination. Whether or not we agree with the political views held by union leaders, on this great issue the American trade union movement has rendered a real service to the cause of freedom.

And I can testify from first hand experience that in many of the countries I have visited in Asia, Africa, and South America, I found the same principle in operation: one of the strongest bulwarks against communism is a strong, free trade union movement.

✻   ✻   ✻   ✻

The Steel Strike: [29] Just before the President left on his trip abroad, he said in his television address to the nation: "It is up to labor and management ... to adjust responsibly and suitably their differences ... what great news it would be if, during the course of this journey, I should receive word of a settlement of this steel controversy that is fair to the workers, fair to management and above all fair to the American people."

The first question that Secretary of Labor Mitchell and I undertook to explore was whether the President's expressed desire for a settlement could be realized without some new mediation action on our part. Our preliminary discussions with representatives of both sides convinced us that there was no chance whatever for a settlement unless some new initiative was undertaken to bring them together.

We, therefore, asked Mr. Blough and other top management representatives and Mr. McDonald and other representatives of the union whether they wished us to attempt to mediate the dispute. While both sides indicated that they did not feel there was too much hope that they could reach a negotiated settlement, they agreed that such a procedure was worth trying and that they would cooperate to the extent possible. This was the origin of the meetings which took place in my home in which Secretary Mitchell, Mr. Blough, Mr. Mc-Donald, Mr. Goldberg, and I participated.

[29] The balance of this section consists of a reprint of the full text of a letter from the Vice President to the editor of the Syracuse, N.Y., *Herald-Journal,* giving an account of the negotiations that led to the steel strike settlement in January 1960, and some general observations on labor-management relations.

At the beginning of these negotiations the possibilities of settlement seemed hopeless. The companies' offer was for a wage-benefit package which the companies estimated would add 31 cents to their cost over a period of thirty months. In addition, the companies asked for revision of Section 2B of the contract so that management would have more control over local work practices, which they felt was essential for increased efficiency.

The union completely opposed any changes in the work practices provision of the contract. On the economic side, Mr. McDonald at our first meeting bluntly stated, "I cannot settle with the steel companies for less than the amount that I received from Can and Aluminum without a strike." I think it is important at this point to recall that our negotiations began the week that he had completed his negotiation of the Aluminum contract. And the companies' computation of what McDonald contended was the Can and Aluminum pattern was an increased wage-benefit cost of 52 cents for thirty months.

In other words, at the beginning of the negotiations, the companies were offering a 31 cents increase over 30 months as against 52 cents demanded by the union, and the parties were in complete disagreement on the local work practices issue. During our first few meetings we made very little progress. At a meeting in my home two days before Christmas, the negotiations reached a point where both sides refused to move any further in the direction of an agreement and there seemed to be a hopeless deadlock.

It was at this point that the Secretary and I talked to Mr. Blough and Mr. McDonald separately and asked whether they thought it might be useful if we were to consult individually with each party and recommend an amount in between their two positions that each would be completely free to accept or reject if he saw fit.

Both agreed that this course of action might be helpful, and after two days of intense negotiations and discussions and consultation with the President we recommended the figure of 41 cents, which both the union and management voluntarily accepted. As far as the work practices issue was concerned, the best that we were able to get the union to agree to was to set up a study commission with a neutral chairman.

I realize that a number of questions have been raised as to why we recommended the amount we did. I think the answers to those questions can be found when we examine the bargaining position of each party.

Mr. McDonald came to these negotiations in a stronger position than the companies. He had just won from Aluminum and Can without a strike higher settlements than the one he eventually agreed to accept with the steel companies. Polls that he had taken (and incidentally, the polls the companies had taken substantiated his claims in this respect) indicated that the union members would vote down the companies' last offer by a majority of over 90 per cent. He also believed that if the disputes were not settled and had to be sent to the Congress by the President he would do better in a Congress heavily dominated by members elected with union support in an election year than would the companies. Considering the strong bargaining position of the union, their agreement to a settlement which was less than the pattern that they had been able to negotiate with Can and Aluminum was, in my opinion, a major achievement.

Looking at the settlement from the standpoint of the companies, no one questions but that they agreed to an amount which was greater than they thought could be absorbed by increased worker productivity, though it is entirely conceivable that the rising efficiency between now and 1962 could offset the increase in labor costs during this period. In addition, the companies failed to win substantial concessions on the work rules issue. But company representatives had pointed out some of these positive factors which led them to agree to the recommended settlement.

1. The amount they settled for was lower than any offer they had been able to get from the union during the course of their negotiations up to that time.

2. It was less than one-half of the postwar pattern in wage-benefit increases in the steel industry. For example, in the last steel contract the wage-benefit increase was 81 cents for three years as compared with 41 cents for thirty months on this occasion.

3. As Conrad Cooper, the chief negotiator for the companies, has stated, the amount of this settlement was 30 per cent less in company costs than would have been the case had Can, Aluminum, and Kaiser patterns been applied to steel. In other words, this settlement rather than setting off a new pattern of higher wage increases was actually lower than the pattern in wage settlements already established in 1959 and checked, rather than increased, the so-called "ripple" of increased wage costs.

4. The cost-of-living escalator provision, which had resulted in a 17-cent wage increase over the three years of the previous contract, was finally limited in this contract to a maximum of 6 cents over thirty months. In addition, it is provided that if the insurance costs which the company has assumed under the contract prove to be greater than the amount estimated, the excess costs will be deducted from any cost-of-living increases which may have accrued.

A basic question which may be raised is whether a better result in the end would have been achieved had the Secretary and I not offered our good offices for mediation of the dispute at this time. This, of course, is a matter of judgment on which there can be an honest disagreement of opinion. I can only indicate my own appraisal as to what would have happened had we not acted as we did.

In my opinion, the price the union would have insisted upon would inevitably have gone up rather than down. It seems only logical to conclude that after the union had won an over-whelming victory rejecting the companies' last offer they would have insisted on an even higher settlement than they accepted at the present time. I also believe that if the parties had failed to agree after the union rejected the companies' last offer and the President, as required by law, had submitted the dispute to Congress, any government-imposed settlement that the Congress would have brought about through compulsory arbitration, plant seizures, or some other government device, would have been higher than the one agreed upon at this point.

I recognize that there are those who have suggested that it would have been better in the long run to allow the issue to go to the Congress so that the Congress could meet head-on the whole question of too much power in the hands of the union as well as management. I can only say that any objective observer would have to agree that there could be nothing more irresponsible than to place before the Congress in an election year the complicated and potentially explosive issue of labor-management relations.

In my opinion, the result not only would have been a government-imposed settlement of this dispute but a real possibility of the enactment of permanent legislation which would have provided for some form of government-imposed compulsory arbitration in all major labor disputes. I do not need to tell you that government arbitration means government wage-fixing and that government wage-fixing inevitably means government price-fixing. Once we get into this vicious circle not only collective bargaining but the productive private enterprise system, as we know it, is doomed.

I would be the last to contend that there could not be honest differences of opinion as to the wisdom of the course of action the Secretary and I followed in mediating this dispute. But after weighing all the factors involved, we concluded that our failure to do everything possible to bring about a voluntary settlement at this time would have been detrimental to the public interest.

As Chairman of the Cabinet Committee on Price Stability for Economic Growth, I am acutely aware of the dangers of inflation which can arise from wage increases that consistently exceed increases in productivity. But on the plus side it should be noted that while the wage-benefit increase was greater than the companies wanted to pay, this was the first contract since the war in which the increase was such that the companies did not find it necessary to increase prices at the time the contract went into force. Whether price increases can be avoided in the future will depend to a great extent upon how the union and the companies carry out the President's injunction in his State of the Union message that ... "the national interest demands that in the period of industrial peace which has been secured by the new contract, both management and labor make every possible effort to increase efficiency and productivity in the manufacture of steel so that price increases can be avoided."

Incidentally, I believe that one of the constructive results of the long fight the companies made on the work rule issue was that it focused nationwide attention on the critical necessity of increasing our efficiency and productivity if we are to maintain our competitive position in the world.

As I told the representatives of the major companies and the union at a dinner in my home after the settlement, the people of the country will not tolerate another massive struggle of this type in the steel industry. Their interest, as well as that of the country at large, will be at stake as they explore every possible means of increasing productivity, reducing costs, and improving relations between union and management during the period of this contract.

For my part, I intend to continue my studies of this problem with a view to determining what legislative action might be taken which would provide better protection for the public interest in the settlement of labor-management disputes and at the same time not impair the basic strength of our private enterprise economy.

6. *Civil Rights* [30]

Reverence for law and due process are among the highest achievements of civilized man. They do not merely protect the rights of minorities against the arbitrary rule of the majority. They protect the very basis of human civilization for majority and minority alike. Their preservation and extension should be among the first concerns of every citizen in a democracy.

But our ideal of democracy goes further even than the protection of our rights and liberties. We also believe in the positive freedom that we call equality of opportunity. We want every American citizen to have an equal chance for a good education, a job that will use his full skills, and enough income to provide adequate housing, medical care, and all the other

[30] The material in this section is derived from the following sources: Remarks before the Forty-first National Convention of the American Legion, Minneapolis, Minnesota. August 25, 1959. Responses to questions at television appearance before the Los Angeles Press Club, Los Angeles, California. February 17, 1959. Remarks to the American Society of Newspaper Editors, Washington, D.C. April 18, 1959. Responses to questions at News Conference, Detroit, Michigan. February 15, 1960. Responses to questions at the Economic Club of Detroit, Detroit, Michigan. February 15, 1960. Remarks at the National Brotherhood Award Dinner of the National Conference of Christians and Jews, Cleveland, Ohio. February 27, 1958. Remarks at the Joint Defense Appeal of the American Jewish Committee and the Anti-Defamation League of B'nai B'rith, Chicago, Illinois. April 30, 1957. Remarks at the Sixty-sixth Annual Convention of the General Federation of Women's Clubs, Asheville, North Carolina. June 5, 1957. Remarks at the Ninety-ninth Annual Commencement, Michigan State University, East Lansing, Michigan. June 9, 1957.

necessities of life. It is not enough to avoid injustice; we must work actively to secure the fullness of justice for all.

We must realize that democracy is indivisible. We cannot have privilege for the few and discrimination for the many. We cannot have one law for the rich and powerful and another for the weak. We cannot teach our children in the schools the glories of our history and the greatness of our democracy if they read in the papers of violence done to those whose only crime is to want the equality that our law guarantees to them.

In every community where racial tensions exist today—and let me emphasize that this problem is not limited to the South —there is need for moderate, constructive action by people of both races. We must not allow the extremists and demagogues to take over this field by default. Nor is it particularly appropriate for some people in the North to point their fingers at the South without dealing effectively with the problem in their own backyards.

It is only through the willingness of public-spirited citizens —in all walks of life, in all sections of the country—to assume personal responsibility for removing the causes of racial prejudice that we can assure the progress that eventually will make the American dream of equality of opportunity a reality for all of our citizens.

It is not enough for us to sit back and say, "Let the government solve this problem." It is true that there are important steps government can take in this field. For example, the enactment of sound and moderate civil rights legislation is one effective step we can take toward living up to our democratic ideals. But there are drawbacks to efforts to achieve racial progress by way of law. Even the most necessary laws are considered by some to be a challenge and an intrusion. Legislation in this area tends to provoke the extremists on both sides. It can have the effect of silencing moderate and constructive elements that have been trying for years—by education and persuasion and the force of example—to bring justice and harmony into our racial picture.

It may take decades to achieve equality of opportunity for our Negro citizens if we rely on Federal law alone. And such an extended struggle could leave a legacy of bitterness which would poison our national life. We must fit the law to the problem at hand. We must not go so far in our legal remedies that we end up passing laws just "for the record," laws with which we do not honestly expect compliance.

One of my professors in law school, a professor in Contracts, made a statement the very first day of school to this effect:

"Gentlemen, there is only one rule or one principle you should remember, if you forget everything else you hear in this course. A contract is only as good as the will of the parties to keep it."

We could draw an analogy here and say that a law is only as good as the will of the people to obey it. This does not mean that we must pass no law until all of the people are ready to obey it. But it does mean that in enacting legislation in a field like this, we must recognize that public support for the law is essential if the law is to be truly effective. And that support must come from the hearts of the people. The people must support it not only because they believe that to obey the law is right but also, eventually, because they believe that the law itself is right. Here is a challenge which in the final analysis must be met by community leaders throughout the nation.

I would not suggest that this is going to be easy.

I attended Duke University for three years, and I can testify from personal experience that the problems impeding integration in the South are real and substantial. At the same time, from an economic standpoint alone, the United States cannot afford not to deal effectively with any problem that deprives 17 million American citizens of the opportunity to develop skills and to make their maximum contribution to our national life.

From a moral standpoint the cause involved is a great one. The battle against bias, bigotry, and discrimination can be equated to upholding the great democratic ideal of liberty under law, and to preserving the fundamental guarantees of the Bill of Rights. No nobler aims could be espoused.

The Administration's policy has not been, is not now, and should not be immediate and total integration.[31] We have to deal with the facts of life as they are. The Administration's position is one which avoids both extremes—the one that says, "We shall do nothing," which means there will be no progress; and the other that tries to do too much, which might result in losing ground rather than gaining it.

Whatever we may think on the issue of civil rights, I believe that the great majority of Americans will agree on this much: there is no legal, moral, or other justification for denying any American the right to vote. The present Administration, recognizing that it cannot change in one year, two years, even five years, customs and practices that have developed over a period of almost a hundred years, has taken a firm position in

[31] The Civil Rights Act of 1960, passed in April, contained these major Administration proposals: (a) voter-referee plan, under which Court-appointed officers will register and guarantee voting rights for all qualified citizens in areas where a "pattern of discrimination" is found to exist; (b) retention for 22 months of all voting records by state and local officials to make possible thorough investigation of alleged denials of voting rights; (c) criminal penalties for obstruction or threats of obstruction to court orders; (d) making bombings and transportation of explosives a federal offense; (e) provision for the education of the children of military personnel in areas where schools have been shut down over the issue of desegregation. Two other proposals were not included in the 1960 Act: (a) making permanent the Cabinet Committee—of which the Vice President is chairman—on job discrimination under federal contracts; and (b) grants-in-aid to school districts penalized by state and local action for attempting to comply with Court-ordered desegregation.

behalf of progress in this area of ensuring every citizen's right to vote. I think this approach offers the best hope for eventual solution of what, to all Americans, is a very difficult and complicated problem.

We believe that in handling this problem we have made some progress without going to extremes. And yet our rate of progress has been criticized by some who honestly believe that other approaches would have been more in the national interest.

I think it would be an exaggeration to say that the school integration program is proceeding at a pace entirely consistent with the 1954 Supreme Court decision. Inevitably this decision has had an effect in some areas of the South of building up massive resistance. We should not be surprised by this.

However, there has been notable progress in several states—Texas, Oklahoma, Kentucky, and North Carolina, for instance. As far as the future is concerned, I believe that the current program of the Administration is the proper one.

As for Federal supervision of elections in the South, I wholeheartedly support the Administration's referee proposal. I believe it is far superior to the well-intentioned but less effective recommendation of the Civil Rights Commission, because the referee proposal will deal not only with registrations, but also with voting itself. After all, what good does it do to be able to register if you cannot vote?

The referee proposal, through judicial processes, guarantees not only the right to register but the right to vote—and not only in Federal elections but in state and local elections as well.

But I think it is well to repeat that the problem of racial relationships will not be solved by a Supreme Court decision or by a new commission. Basically it must be solved in the minds and hearts of people. People in positions of responsibility and leadership—business leaders, educational leaders, political leaders—have to create the climate in which we not only have a law on the books, but also the will within the minds and hearts of the people to obey this law.

In the worldwide struggle in which we are engaged, racial and religious prejudice is a gun we point at ourselves.

We cannot preach brotherhood to peoples abroad and practice bigotry and prejudice at home. Our enemies magnify the smallest incident for all the world to see. The effectiveness of this magnified distortion is, unfortunately, all too great. We have seen it in Formosa, in Viet Nam, in other lands. Shall we blame the Formosans or the Vietnamese? I do not believe we can. Part of the blame belongs to us. We can blame the Communists for exploiting every opportunity, but first we need to look within our own hearts.

I have been in nearly every one of the countries of Asia, most of those in Africa, and some in the Near East. In this great complex of countries there are approximately a billion people—about one-third of the world's population. They constitute the so-called neutral world. To judge by the welcome that President Eisenhower received from them, their hearts are on the side of freedom.

But these people want not only independence and economic progress; they also want recognition of their individual dignity as human beings.

Each of these countries is different in religion, dress, and language, but they are alike in one respect: 95 per cent of their people are nonwhite. Thus every instance of mistreatment or denial of rights to nonwhite citizens in this country is blown up a thousandfold. I know of nothing that does more harm to United States foreign policy abroad than incidents of this type. I can only say, and from considerable personal experience, that it is most difficult for a representative of this country to talk one way abroad and then to explain some of our contradictory practices at home.

We can tell them, as we do, that we respect their dignity and that we consider them to be our moral, political, and social equals. But the impression people abroad have of America is determined more by what we do than what we say. And the question that is inevitably asked in Asia, in Africa, and in the Near East is: do you really believe in equality when you practice racial discrimination in your own country?

It is only natural that this "neutral" world is putting us under a microscope to examine our flaws and imperfections. Millions of people newly freed from colonial rule must now decide their future course. They have known too long the stigma of inferiority to be tolerant of injustice and prejudice. It is not too much to say that our devotion to the cause of world freedom will be judged almost exclusively, by these nations, in terms of our practical devotion to the ideal of equality at home. If we fail here, regardless of our other virtues, we may be found wanting.

The Kremlin propagandists seize upon every failure of the Western world to live up to its ideals of liberty under law. They enormously exaggerate these incidents and broadcast them within their empire and to the millions in Asia and Africa. They particularly attack the United States as a land groaning under exploitation and discrimination—a mixture of the money-mad few and the poverty-stricken many. This is a caricature, of course, but it is most important that we do not feed Red propagandists raw material for such caricatures. I could give example after example of how instances of prejudice and discrimination in the United States have been used devastatingly against us in countries abroad.

It follows then that whenever we contribute to the elimination of prejudice and discrimination in the United States we not only help those discriminated against; we serve the cause of freedom, worldwide, and strike an effective blow against communism and all forms of dictatorship.

What can we do?

We must practice equality at home as effectively as we talk it abroad.

We must be more judicious and selective in the people we send overseas.

Our tourists should be better briefed on our national problems abroad.

We must have more people from abroad see us as we are at home.

We must do a far more effective job in telling the true story of our progress toward brotherhood.

And we have made some real progress. The very fact that Americans are so concerned about denial of voting rights, denial of adequate education, denial of employment opportunities to our Negro citizens is, itself, a sure sign of progress.

The truth is America's most potent weapon. We cannot enlarge upon the truth. But we can and must intensify our efforts to make that truth more shining.

7.   *Forgotten Peoples* [32]

Generally speaking, the American people and our government have a long and honorable tradition, insofar as our attitude toward refugees is concerned. There have been some exceptions, but when we look over the history of this country from the very beginning, our people and our government have opened their hearts, their homes, and their pocketbooks to people in distress, wherever they may be in the world.

[32] The material in this section is derived from the Vice President's Address to the White House Refugee Meeting, Washington, D.C. May 21, 1959.

For example, since World War II we have appropriated and spent over a billion dollars in behalf of refugees and have admitted to this country over 700,000 refugees. At the present time approximately 25 to 30 per cent of the care for refugees throughout the world is furnished by the United States. These facts indicate that our long tradition of concern for refugees is continuing during the present period.

A very dramatic indication of this was the American people's response to the Hungarian revolution and resulting refugee problem. When we consider the sudden nature and the magnitude of the problem, I think that the record of our people, of our voluntary organizations, and of our government was one of which we can justly be proud.

Having commented about the areas in which the United States and its people can point with pride, may I also suggest a criticism and offer an observation with regard to the American character.

Whenever we have a problem, whether it is refugees or foreign aid, or even a domestic problem such as the building of a highway or a school, we like to solve it in a hurry. Unless we are able to see the end of the road, unless we are able to accomplish our objective within a reasonable length of time, we tend to tire and to switch to some other activity which will inspire us and take our minds off of what might have been an even more important job which we have just left unfinished. I do not need to tell you that that is exactly the situation with regard to the world refugee problem.

In December of 1956, I visited Austria—which was as close to the Hungarian situation as I could get. I shall never forget the tremendous reaction of the American people upon my return and their response to the volunteer societies' request for funds. General Gruenther, the president of the American Red Cross, told me that in recent years the Red Cross has never had a drive which was more successful than this one which prompted Americans to contribute so generously to refugees from Hungary. But now time has passed and we have a tendency to feel that this job is done—or if it is not, it should be. And this brings me to the point I want to emphasize.

The American people must remember the magnitude of the problem that we still have to solve with regard to refugees throughout the world. Speaking in terms of numbers, the estimates run anywhere from 2,300,000, which is the hard core of refugees, up to 15,000,000.

But let us speak in human terms of the lives and characteristics of the refugees still living in countries in which they do not have the equal rights and privileges of citizens. I saw them firsthand when I visited refugee camps in Austria and in Germany. I am not referring now to the recent refugees, the Hungarians. There was no particular problem in getting countries to accept them and in finding homes and funds for them. I am speaking about the people who have been in camps for ten years, older people, people suffering from some disability which should not but does disqualify them from entry into the United States and other countries.

The longer they remain in these camps, the more hopeless the future becomes for them and for their children. Therefore, although this hard-core figure of 2,300,000 is not as exciting as the hordes of refugees that poured across the border at Andau as I saw them in December, 1956, their problem should really touch our hearts even more; they have suffered long, and they need all the help that we can give—not just food and clothing and housing, but care and personal attention. Eventually, they need new homes in countries in which they can live on an equal basis with those around them.

Some action on the part of our government is needed—some action in addition to what we are already doing. Government action is necessary because the problem is so big. It is necessary, for instance, where immigration laws must be modified in order to provide the homes that are required. But it is not my intention at this point to make explicit recommendations as to what that action should be.

Rather, the point that I would like to emphasize here is that the refugee problem is not just a problem for government. It is a problem for people, for volunteer organizations and for individuals. I have visited camps in Hong Kong, in Viet Nam, in Korea, in Pakistan, in Austria, and in Germany. In camp after camp I was tremendously impressed by the contribution that was being made by the volunteer American organizations. They were providing what government could never provide, a sincere, personalized interest in the individual as distinguished from the statistic.

There is another reason why the problem of refugees must concern the American people. It relates to the image that we present to the world.

Many of us have heard about and read the controversial book *The Ugly American*. It is not my province here to comment on whether or not that book adequately or accurately portrays what the United States is doing abroad. But if nothing else, the book did stimulate discussion as to whether people of other countries have an accurate picture of what truly is the attitude of the United States and what our interests in them are. In this great world conflict we constantly have to find ways and means to destroy damaging pictures of the United States that are presented by our opponents in the world, and to project on an affirmative basis a true picture of the United States.

Now what does our attitude toward refugees have to do with this? And, particularly, what does the concern for refugees displayed by individuals and private volunteer organizations have to do with the image or picture of America? Simply this: Too often, where our foreign aid program, for example, or our Mutual Security Program is concerned, people abroad get the impression that the sole interest of the United States in Pakistan, in India, in the people of Africa, or Latin America, or

Indonesia, is self-interest—that we help them only because we want them on our side, and because we are afraid if we do not help them they will go over to the Communist side.

Now there is and must be self-interest in the Mutual Security Programs of the United States, in our Development Loan Fund Program, and in the various other assistance programs in which we engage. But it is not true of either the government of the United States or the people of the United States that we help less fortunate people abroad solely because of self-interest. Even if there were no communism in the world, there would still be hunger and misery and disease, and we would be concerned. And this is the point we must get across.

We can get it across, to some extent, by means of information programs and by what individual Americans say and do when they go abroad. But no one activity more accurately presents the true heart of America than the work with refugees undertaken by American volunteer organizations. The contributions of the American people—their dollars, their time, their energy—channeled through these organizations are made not in the interest of the foreign policy of the United States, but because it is traditional and right for us in this New World to work for those who are less fortunate, wherever they may be, any place in the world.

PART FIVE

Mission to the Soviet Union

1. *Russia as I Saw It* [33]

It was less than twenty-four hours after my arrival in Moscow that I got my first striking lesson in Soviet determination—in their driving purpose to achieve for themselves a better and more abundant life—and a lesson in Soviet logic as well.

I had already been impressed, while driving from the airport to the center of the city, by the astonishing amount of new building, most of it huge apartments aimed at relieving the chronic Soviet housing shortage that is still far from beaten. Then, right at the start of the "great debate" [34] with Premier Khrushchev in the television studios of the American National Exhibition at Sokolniki Park, he turned to me and said:

"We wish you success in showing what America is capable of. How long has America existed—three hundred years?"

"More than a hundred and fifty," I told him.

"Well, then," he went on, "we will say America has been in existence for a hundred and fifty years, and this is the level she has reached. We have existed not quite forty-two years and in another seven we will be on the same level as America." And he said that then they would pass us by and go further still!

Now, nothing I saw during my eleven days in the Soviet Union—and let me say at once that I don't believe this makes me, overnight, a "Russian expert"—none of the sharp impressions I carried away leads me to believe that they will equal our standard of living in seven years—or in seventy—if only we remain true to the traditions that have made possible our fabulous growth up to now.

---

[33] "Russia as I Saw It" by Richard M. Nixon first appeared in the *National Geographic* Magazine, Volume CXVI, No. 6, December, 1959. Copyright © 1959 by the National Geographic Society. Reprinted by permission.

[34] For extended excerpts from this debate, see below pp. 219–227.

But I *was* impressed by Premier Khrushchev's determination, by his evident deep belief in the future development of the Soviet Union's vast potential, by the intense purposefulness of Soviet leaders and Soviet people alike to make this potential real. And I couldn't help noticing, too, his curious offhand assumption that all of Russian history worth mentioning dates back only to the Revolution of 1917!

The most important point, though, is this: no matter how great the potential Soviet challenge, this very Soviet determination to achieve a better and richer life opens the possibility at the same time for a great hope. Such a life can flourish only in an atmosphere of peace, of mutual cooperation among nations and peoples—and this is a hope that I tried, over and over again, to exploit in all my contacts with the Soviet leaders and people. But more of that later.

I was not in Moscow, of course, to debate with Premier Khrushchev. I was there, as President Eisenhower's official representative, to open the American National Exhibition, and, at the same time, to talk candidly with the Soviet leaders, to learn as much as I could about their land and people, to help relieve in some small way the appalling misinformation—among leaders and people alike—about America and its purposes and goals.

With what success? Obviously, I cannot say. But I think I can say this much at least: That America will leave unexplored no avenue that might conceivably lead the way, eventually, to an honorable and enduring peace. And that was the heart of my own message to the Soviet people.

The Exhibition itself was a tremendous success. It was designed to show some of the things we produce under our free-enterprise system, and something, too, of the quality of American life. As I put it in my radio-TV address to the Soviet people, how nearly we in America have achieved freedom and abundance for all in a classless society—the very goal that the Communists claim as their own special property!

I think the Soviet people were impressed. Millions of them visited the Exhibition—the unofficial attendance figures were 3 million—and when I was in Moscow, tickets to the fair were about the most highly prized possessions in town.

That scarcity of tickets, in fact, gave Soviet officials a chance to try some malicious anti-American propaganda at my expense. It happened the day after I arrived in Moscow.

I woke up early and, with one of my staff and an interpreter, drove down to the Danilovskiy farmer's market. This is a fascinating place, mostly open-air, with hundreds of small stands selling fruits and vegetables, flowers and herbs, everything, in fact, from plastic toys to fresh milk. Such places have always held a special fascination for me—dating all the way back to my school days when I was in charge of the produce department of our family grocery and used to drive early every morning to the Los Angeles wholesale market to buy the day's supplies.

Everyone at the market—vendors and customers—was very friendly, and, when they learned who I was, at every stand where I stopped they insisted I sample their products and flatly refused any money. When I left, one of the women selling flowers gave me a bouquet as a gift from all the vendors.

But just before we left, several people asked me for tickets to the Exhibition, scheduled to open later that day. I told them I had none with me, but I called over the man who said he was director of the market and said I should be glad to give him money to buy tickets for everyone. But he assured me it was not the one-ruble price that stood in their way; tickets simply were unobtainable. We promised to do what we could to help.

The next morning Moscow's *Trud* carried an indignant letter, charging in effect that I was up to the usual "capitalist tricks," that I had sought out ill-dressed Russian workers and tried to get one to accept money so photographers could take pictures of the incident and send them around the world!

I'm happy to report, however, that this completely false story did not appear to do much harm to the cause of Soviet-American friendship. One of the journalists in our party went to the market next morning with a photographer. He chatted informally with vendors and customers. And later he told me this amusing and revealing story.

"They couldn't have been nicer," he said. "Everyone was talking about your visit and seemed very pleased with it. When I told them I was an American, one of the flower vendors insisted on giving me a bouquet of carnations. Three more followed suit. I tried to refuse, but they insisted.

"I've spent a good deal of time in markets like that one, and I've found that people like it if you eat something that's on sale there. Well, the only thing available at the moment was a big barrel of dill pickles. I picked out a nice pickle and tried to buy it, but they wouldn't take my money. The stallkeeper insisted I take it as a gift. So I thanked her and ate it. It was delicious.

"I went on through the market, and everywhere I stopped, people would gather to assure me of their desire for peace and friendship. The only trouble was that word had gotten around that I liked dill pickles. Every time I passed a stand where they were available—and this is the season—someone insisted on making me a present!"

The official count, before the photographer finished his work: four large pickles consumed in the cause of Soviet-American friendship.

"We left in a great surge of good feeling," the journalist concluded. "I had my tape recorder over one shoulder, two cameras around my neck, a gadget bag over the other shoulder, four bunches of carnations in one hand—and a dill pickle in the other! If these people don't like Americans, they have funny ways of showing it!"

Now of course this is a small enough incident, not especially important in itself. But it does serve to point up the great truth that the Russian people *do* like Americans. Everywhere we went in the Soviet Union, the impression was the same— an atmosphere of friendship, respect, admiration, and curiosity about everyone and everything American.

The Russian people may be skeptical about the living standard of the average American worker; after all, this is out of the range of their wildest dreams. But if the Soviet government has failed in anything, it has most spectacularly failed in forty years of unremitting propaganda to convince the Russian people that Americans are warmongers and oppressors. Their friendship seemed to be as real as it was spontaneous and heart-warming.

That is why the Exhibition was so important. President Eisenhower called the $3,600,000 we spent on the fair "about the best investment the government has made in a long time." Those of us who saw it, and saw the popular response to it, could not agree more.

Someone called the 400,000-square-foot exhibit in Sokolniki Park "a corner of America in the heart of Moscow." And that was indeed the purpose. It was not a trade fair, not just a display of products, but a demonstration of the incredible richness and the wonderful variety of American life.

President Eisenhower, in his preface to the official guidebook, summed up our hopes this way:

"It is my fervent wish that by this means, and through the corresponding Exhibition which your country is holding in New York City, the people of our two great nations may gain a better understanding of one another. Thus can the foundations be strengthened for our cooperation in the achievement of mankind's greatest goal—a fruitful and flourishing world at peace."

One of the most striking facts about the fair was that the visitors were almost more interested in the American guides than they were in the American goods. Day after day these seventy-five carefully chosen bilingual young people—twenty-seven girls among them—were surrounded by hundreds of visitors, all eager to know about life in America.

"How much does the average American earn?" "What is your monthly rent?" "How does an American live when he is unemployed?" "Do you own a car?" These are only samples of the questions with which our guides were deluged. They gave honest and unrehearsed answers, too, answers that made no attempt to cover up our shortcomings, but rather told all the truth of American life. And they were themselves excellent representatives of the whole American people.

There were literally thousands of government officials, exhibitors, and workmen who also contributed greatly to the success of the Exhibition. But one man in particular deserves to be singled out; he deserves, too, the eternal gratitude of the American people for his superb job in overcoming near-insurmountable obstacles and seeing to it that the fair opened right on schedule. That man is Harold "Chad" McClellan, a mild-mannered but tough-minded Los Angeles businessman who was general manager of the Exhibition.

The visitors to the fair probably saw and felt more of America than I did of Moscow. Courtesy calls, official and formal meetings and engagements, the preparation of speeches—all this took too much of my time. I did manage to get away for a brief walk through the streets shortly after my arrival, and, passing a *Gastronom*, a government grocery store, I dropped in for a little comparison shopping.

Even at the favorable tourist rate of 10 rubles to the dollar, food is expensive. Butter, for example, was $1.20 a pound, and ordinary yellow cheese $1.40. A can of plums was priced at $1.10, one of peaches higher still. The few imported items were fantastically high: a 2-ounce tin of instant coffee cost $4. Fresh caviar was $8.50 a pound. And the average Soviet worker earns but $80 a month!

My wife Pat had a better chance than I to see the city. She visited the First Children's Hospital and a nursery school, leaving behind her a trail of candy and chewing gum. She also toured the Botanical Gardens, where she presented the director with two dogwoods that we had brought as gifts from the United States. In return, the Russians filled her arms with orchids and roses—all of which contributed to making our rooms at Spaso House, where we were guests of Ambassador Llewellyn Thompson, Jr., and his charming wife, into a fair substitute for a florist shop.

Our effort to see the Soviet Union really only got started when, in our jet cavalcade of three new Soviet Tu-104B's, we flew to Leningrad. The 500-mile-an-hour planes made the trip in less than an hour, but when we got off at Leningrad airport, I thought for a minute that by some mistake we had flown home instead. There were dozens of American tourists in the crowd, several of them waving home-made welcome signs.

Leningrad itself, the second-largest Soviet city and its chief seaport, is a place of great beauty and charm. The scars of its long wartime siege are still visible, but there is evidence everywhere of rebuilding and new construction. Like so much of this throughout the Soviet Union, though, the new buildings— at least to an American—tend to a monotonous similarity.

Peter the Great built the city in the early eighteenth century as a "window on Europe," and the architecture, nearly all of it in stone, was deliberately Western in style.

It was Peter's own castle, Petrodvorets, that impressed me most. Frol R. Kozlov, the Soviet First Deputy Premier, was my host, and together we toured this fantastic estate which was once the home of the Tsars.

Peter was evidently an accomplished practical joker. The grounds of the castle are filled with fountains, and the unwary or uninitiated are in constant danger of a thorough soaking.

There is, for example, a bench conveniently placed for enjoying the superb view. When you sit on it, though, a well-directed spray drenches both bench and occupant. There is also a tree where the visitor gets an unexpected shower.

Mr. Kozlov and I escaped dry, but an overenthusiastic caretaker, eager to show off the mechanism, turned on the jet before everyone was in the clear. Georgi K. Zhukov, chairman of the State Committee for Cultural Relations Abroad, was completely drenched.

"This is a pretty good way to cool off hot-heads," I told him. "We might do well to use it a little more often in diplomacy."

Again, let me say that I tell you this story not for its own sake and not because it proves a great deal. But it does indicate the many, many ways in which Russians and Americans are, as people, basically alike. We can, at least, laugh at the same things. The problem is to find more, and more important, similarities—and then exploit them as avenues to the peaceful cooperation of our two great peoples.

It was at Petrodvorets that I met an attractive pig-tailed schoolgirl who joined our inspection party. I asked her what she wanted to be when she grew up.

"I'm going to be a schoolteacher," she said.

I told her I thought that was a pretty good idea; my wife had been a schoolteacher herself when we were married.

"What does she do now?" asked an older woman in the crowd.

"Being the wife of the Vice President is a full-time job," I told her.

It's the rule rather than the exception, of course, for Soviet women to work: even in the steel mills and heavy-machinery plants, many women work side by side with men. And this is the case, basically, because of the manpower shortage resulting from the Soviet Union's staggering losses in World War II and because right now the Soviet economy is being driven at maximum wartime capacity rather than at a more leisurely peacetime pace.

Pat visited Petrodvorets with me, but I think she was far more impressed with the hours she spent in the Hermitage, one of the world's great museums. Leningrad has more than fifty museums, including one of Europe's finest natural history collections, but the Hermitage is in a class by itself.

Its six buildings, I was told, have more than 1,500 rooms with more than 2 million items on display. It houses one of the world's leading collections of Western paintings and sculpture, including a matchless group of French Impressionists that has only recently been taken out of storage and put on public display. And its classical, Scythian, and Egyptian exhibits rank with the world's finest. Rembrandts, Rubenses, and Titians also hang in great profusion.

Pat was particularly interested in a woven rug, red and green in color, decorated with figures of horses and reindeer. It was found only recently in a Siberian burial mound, but it still preserves the brilliant color it had when woven 2,500 years ago.

"I wish Tricia and Julie could have been with me," Pat told me later. "One of the most fascinating things in the museum is a wonderful little set of toy furniture. It was made in France in the seventeenth century, of silver filigree set with precious stones. The guide said it was used by the children of the Tsars. The girls would have loved it."

Pat and I, together with Dr. Milton Eisenhower, the President's brother, were guests that night at the Kirov opera house for a performance of *Spartacus*. During the intermission the mayor of Leningrad, or the Soviet equivalent of one, introduced us to the audience, and to our surprise everyone stood and applauded. It was a heart-warming reception, not so much for us as individuals, but for all the American people whom we represented. And again, I am convinced that this typical demonstration was sincere and spontaneous on the part of the Russian people.

The theater itself is a lavish baroque structure, decorated

with gilt frescoes, crystal chandeliers, and countless cupids. I was intrigued by the fact that although the conductor was formally dressed in white tie and tails, most of the orchestra were in shirt sleeves and without neckties—another curious example of the Soviet mixture of the rough and the polished, the old culture and the new. And let me add, too, that the orchestra was excellent. The Soviet emphasis, in every aspect of life, seems to be on practical results, not on refinements.

This was just as true, we found, in a rather more important field. Next day at one of the city's numerous shipyards we inspected the new atomic-powered icebreaker, the *Lenin*. Vice Admiral Hyman G. Rickover, the father of our atomic submarines, was in the party.

Mr. Kozlov, on his tour of the United States, had closely examined one of our atomic-powered ships. We insisted on the same privilege, and Admiral Rickover went over the *Lenin*, especially its power plant, carefully. He felt generally that the basic engineering of this ship, which sailed on her maiden voyage in September, is sound, but does not break any significant new ground.

When we emerged from below decks, we found a crowd of shipyard workers, eager to shake hands and ready with questions. I told them how delighted I was to see atomic energy being put to peaceful use, and they applauded when I added that I would prefer to see all atomic power—and all our skills and resources—directed to the benefit of man, not to his destruction.

"We must remember," I told them, "that in Alaska, Russia and America are only 53 miles apart. That isn't much for an icebreaker like this to handle. But we must all work together to break the diplomatic ice between our governments."

As our trip went on, we could sense from day to day a warming in the climate that surrounded our party. The Soviet press, while never exactly enthusiastic, became less and less critical. And the crowds everywhere grew larger and friendlier. We might, at that, have been doing some "ice-breaking" of our own.

I was especially curious about our reception in the so-called "closed cities" of Siberia, next on the schedule, where few Americans have ever been seen. Certainly, as we headed into Novosibirsk airport, there was nothing in the air view to remind us of our traditional notion of Siberia as arid and barren and forbidding. The countryside was lush and flat, a typical checkerboard of green and yellow and the black of freshly turned fields.

The crowd at the airport was easily the largest we had yet seen. And the city officials who greeted us pointed out with considerable pride that theirs was a new and young and vigorous city, comparable to the cities of our own American West. It certainly could boast of the same tradition of warm hospitality.

It was interesting to note that these officials themselves repeatedly referred to Novosibirsk as the "Chicago of the Soviet Union"—interesting in two ways. First of all, as a further indication of the widespread respect for American growth and progress that we found everywhere in the Soviet Union, and second, as another sign that America is the conscious target of their own efforts. I was told proudly by several officials that they fully expect to surpass Chicago within twenty years—quite a goal when we realize that Novosibirsk is today a city of about 900,000 compared to Chicago's nearly 4 million, and therefore has a long way to go.

The Novosibirsk airport is about 15 miles from town, and all along the road there were groups of people waving and calling out their welcomes—many in the doorways of their log houses, and others working in potato patches and fields of sunflowers. The Russians, I was told, extract cooking oil from sunflower seeds.

Once in the city, we found the streets literally lined with crowds. One bus carrying a load of reporters and photographers took a wrong turn and got back on the route ahead of the official party. It was immediately surrounded by a milling, cheering crowd which very nearly overturned it in its enthusiasm.

When our cavalcade reached Stalin Square, in the heart of the city, the friendly throng broke through the police lines— no mean feat in the Soviet Union—to shake our hands and ask questions.

Novosibirsk is especially proud of its growing industry, and our hosts took us directly to their largest machine-tool plant, the Yefremov factory. We were told that its products are exported principally to China and the European satellites.

I was surprised to note that roughly half the machines in the factory were American-made. Many of the rest bore German markings. One of the correspondents with us, who had spent the postwar years in China, noticed that one of the Cincinnati-made machines carried an instruction plate in Japanese.

Knowing that the Soviets had sacked the Manchurian factories during their "caretaker" occupation of that Chinese province, he asked the foreman if the machine had in fact come from Manchuria.

"No," he was told. "It was one of the machines we bought from you during the war."

"How does it happen to have this Japanese plate?" the reporter persisted.

The foreman shrugged and laughed, "Who knows why Americans do anything?"

The correspondent gave up on that one, but the remark about the "machines we bought from you during the war" started him off on a further line of questioning. He asked, in all, seven subforemen and twelve workers if they knew the approximate value of American lend-lease aid to Russia during the war. Not only did none of them know the amount—in round figures, 11 billion dollars—none of them had even heard of lend-lease! These machines had all been "bought" from the United States during the war!

That night we went to a superb performance of *Swan Lake* in the Novosibirsk opera house, another reminder of the similarities between this Siberian frontier and our own West. If classical ballet in a Siberian city—where many of the houses are still rude log cabins and where modern plumbing is by no means common—seems unusual to you, recall that in mid-nineteenth-century San Francisco, for example, there was this same combination of raw but dynamic vitality and a hunger for culture.

The opera house in Novosibirsk is, in fact, larger even than Moscow's Bolshoi Theater. It is an elaborate amphitheater, built during the darkest days of World War II at a time when housing was in critically short supply.

I was not the first American Vice President to visit there, I later discovered. During his trans-Asian tour in 1944, Henry A. Wallace, then Vice President, spoke in this same opera house, which was then unfinished but was opened especially for him.

Here again, after a magnificent performance, we were treated to typical Soviet and Siberian hospitality. Hundreds of members of the audience crowded around our party to shake hands. When we were escorted backstage to meet the company, we were, as always, deluged with questions about life in America and repeatedly assured that the Soviet people want only *"mir i druzhba"*—peace and friendship—with America.

I couldn't help being struck that evening by the sense in which culture and all the arts are, in themselves, an international language. Van Cliburn is practically a household name in the Soviet Union. And when I mentioned in passing that back home I had recordings of several Tchaikovsky ballets by the London Symphony and by Eugene Ormandy's Philadelphia Orchestra, the crowd was way ahead of the translators. They nodded and smiled in instant recognition of these names, as familiar to them as to any American. Especially after this summer, the mention of Leonard Bernstein and the New York Philharmonic would doubtless get the same response.

I came away all the more convinced by this incident, added to the great success of the Moscow Exhibition, that we need to increase dramatically our cultural and person-to-person exchange programs with the Iron Curtain countries. The people of these countries will inevitably increase their pressures for more consumer goods and for greater freedom from oppressive controls as they become acquainted with the aspects of a richer and freer life through direct contacts with the West.

We drove 18 miles south the next morning to visit the new Novosibirsk hydroelectric power plant, a gigantic installation on the Ob' River with a projected capacity of 400,000 kilowatts. The 3-mile-long dam will form a lake 134 miles long and 12 miles wide. A labor force of more than 70,000, we were told, is at work on the project.

At this dam site I ran into what our traveling press party described as my first Siberian "hecklers." I couldn't prove, of course, that they were planted, or that they were primed with loaded questions, but the uniformity of the questions and of the very words used was too much for coincidence.

One of the most ambitious projects in Novosibirsk is the so-called Scientific Center, still under construction a few miles south of the city. Here, by 1962, the Soviets hope to have a city —estimates range all the way from 15,000 to 60,000—chiefly of scientists, built around a new university and a series of research institutions in such fields as nuclear physics, thermophysics, hydrodynamics, kinetics, and electrometry. Building is going on full steam by a labor force of about 7,000.

As we neared the city on our return trip, I noticed hundreds of little one-room wooden structures set in the middle of small garden plots. One of my hosts explained that they were for "weekend farmers"—city workers who were allowed to till an acre or so of land for their own use and who slept in these rough shelters.

I found tremendous pride among the people of Novosibirsk in their city's rapid growth from its start among birch forests only sixty-six years ago to become the metropolis of Siberia. It has more than doubled in size in the last twenty years.

Geography has played a big part in this success story. Novosibirsk lies on the Ob', at the narrowest part of the river valley, thus at the logical crossing for the Trans-Siberian Railway. The completion of the Altai Railway from the south in 1915 gave a fresh impetus to the city's growth, and foundries and metal-working plants were established to draw on the vast natural resources of the region.

Then, in the 1930s, industrial plants were added, a growth further stimulated during World War II when many factories were moved inland ahead of Hitler's armies. Located at the junction of Siberian water and rail transportation, it was the logical site for the Soviet Union's Siberian arsenal.

Since the war there has been an important change in this industrial complex. Novosibirsk has become one of the country's chief machine-building cities, the center for iron and steel and chemicals, and the unchallenged center of Siberian education and culture as well.

There are nine institutions of higher learning scattered among the factories which now line both banks of the Ob', and Siberia's largest publishing house turns out a stream of books and magazines and newspapers. Here, too, are Siberia's telecasting center, two museums, and a State Conservatory of Music.

Not only is Siberia the center of great industrial growth; members of our embassy staff told me that the "new lands" program, started in 1954, has been concentrated in Siberia and adjoining Kazakhstan. In these five years more than 90 million acres have been brought under cultivation for the first time— a great part of it in wheat.

This new acreage means that some of the rich lands of the Ukraine can be turned from small grain production to corn, which in turn means more meat in a Soviet diet that has run heavily to bread, potatoes, and vegetables. The area of the new lands has a climate very like that of western Canada. The growing season is short, and rainfall seldom exceeds 12 to 14 inches a year. Fortunately, it usually comes at the right time.

Still, farming in the new lands is risky, and results have not been entirely favorable. Last year, for example, a freak August snowfall ruined a good crop in some areas.

People were encouraged to settle the new lands, I was told, by offers of free transportation and interest-free loans for live-stock and homes. Many were "volunteers" from Communist youth organizations, and large numbers of students spent summer vacations helping break out the new lands.

Successful or not, there is little chance that this program can be duplicated. Although the Soviet Union is an enormous country—nearly three times the area of the United States—only about 10 per cent of it is arable; the rest is simply too cold or too dry for farming. Thus the 1954–1959 increase in cultivation used up just about all the land there is.

Then, too, some of the crops produced have been wasted because of administrative blunders. There is a lack of storage elevators, and the road system is inadequate for transport. This means that much of the crop in good years has to be stored on open ground and is lost in bad weather. In 1958, a good crop year, there was a standard joke among the farmers. They said, "We would gladly trade a ton of wheat for just one bottle of vodka. At least we could put the vodka to some use."

We must remember that fully 40 per cent of the Soviet Union's labor force works at agriculture, that it takes one person to produce food for himself and about four other Soviet citizens. Contrast this with the American average of one to twenty-two, and you have some idea of how far the Soviet Union still has to go in turning itself into an industrial nation.

And while both the Soviet Union and the United States have farm problems, ours fortunately is mostly one of surpluses. With but 7½ million farmers and farm workers as against roughly 40 million in the Soviet Union, our over-all output of farm products is much greater. Not only that, of course, but because of our unparalleled technology and capital equipment we exceed Soviet production on much less acreage.

We were all sorry to leave Novosibirsk. It may be raw and rough in many respects, but it is a dynamic and exciting place to be, and tremendously warm at heart. It also happens to produce two table specialties which many of the members of our party found delectable. One is a spicy soup called *ukha*, made from a white fish which is native to the Ob'. The other is a ball of highly seasoned meat encased in a thin coat of pastry and then simmered. Sturdy Siberians think nothing of putting away a couple of dozen of these *pel'meni* at a meal, even at breakfast!

Sverdlovsk was our last stop in Siberia. It lies almost exactly halfway between Moscow and Novosibirsk and is called the industrial capital of the Urals. But it is no mountain city. The Urals resemble our own Catskills much more than the Rockies, and Sverdlovsk is located in gently rolling country, none of it more than 1,000 feet above sea level.

It is the mineral wealth of these mountains, though, that gave Sverdlovsk its start back in 1723 and that has made it into a teeming, smoky city of nearly 800,000 today. It is a center for the processing of iron, copper, tungsten, platinum, gold, and asbestos, and one of the leading Soviet armament centers.

We were again greeted by enthusiastic crowds at the airport, and cheering groups were scattered all along our nine-mile route into town.

Much of the countryside is covered with well-tended pine forest, and most of the cleared land is planted in potatoes. Almost all the houses are log-built, but nearly every window displayed its pots of geraniums and nasturtiums. Even in the city itself most of the houses are built of logs.

Our first full day in Sverdlovsk was a typically busy one. We drove over rolling countryside to Pervoural'sk, where we toured a tube-rolling mill, one of the largest in the Soviet Union. There I was once again struck by the number of women at work and by the inevitable posters which covered nearly every square inch of wall space, urging workers to produce more, reminding them that only communism can lead them to a better life, admonishing them to avoid accidents.

This last warning was certainly necessary. Safety standards in that plant, as in all I visited, were far below those of American factories. Workers drawing hot metal wore no goggles, machine belts were unprotected, and men stacking heavy pigs of metal had no safety shoes.

The young manager seemed to be typical of middle-level Soviet executives; he had started as a worker, studied at night, and finally worked up through the ranks. He had spent a year in America, ten years ago, inspecting material and heavy equipment later purchased by the Soviet Union.

Much of the equipment was old-fashioned by American standards, and there was little evidence of automation. But one of our Intourist girls, an interpreter assigned to the press corps, had never seen a steel mill and was convinced that this must be the last word.

"I'm sure you don't have anything like that in America," she said proudly to one of the American newsmen.

"Not any more," he answered, and left her looking very puzzled indeed.

But let us make no mistake about it. We may today be well ahead of the Soviet Union in automation, plant capacity, and capital equipment, but they are making an almost superhuman effort to catch up, and even surpass us. They are dead serious about their goals. And so there is only one way for us to stay ahead—we must constantly move forward.

Before we reached the tube mill, however, we had passed quite a landmark: the frontier between Europe and Asia. A concrete obelisk marks the spot. Picnic tables had been set up, complete with a supply of well-chilled champagne, so that we could toast the occasion. I remarked that I was exactly halfway around the world from my own home in California, and that the shortest way there would be straight through the earth.

My hosts evidently took me at my word. For when we reached the Degtyarsk copper mine after lunch, I found myself fitted out in heavy working clothes and miner's cap and lamp, 800 feet below ground in the mine, talking with two miners about the problems of controlling atomic tests and of enforcing any ban on such testing.

One of the miners very seriously put this question to me:

"You say you do not want war, but why then do you keep on with your atomic tests? Why don't you stop them?"

"This is the best place in the world for you to ask me that question," I answered. "What we in America are interested in is not simply an agreement to stop these tests but an agreement that can be enforced, that both sides will adhere to. Did you know that tests can now be conducted underground, as far below the surface as we are right now, which cannot be detected unless you have inspectors right on the spot? That is why we insist on an inspection system that will give both of us the assurance that any agreement we sign is being lived up to."

I think this argument—which he clearly had never heard

before—really hit home. At any rate, I was most impressed by the miners' serious approach to these problems, and as I left I made the suggestion: "You men are in the wrong profession. You should be statesmen."

"But then who would do the mining?" one of them replied.

Pat was meanwhile doing some visiting of her own. Mrs. Valya Kalyagina, the wife of one of the miners, asked her to come to her home, where they spent a pleasant hour together and were entertained with a few accordion solos by Mrs. Kalyagina's husband.

Pat also had a busy time in Sverdlovsk, and I think the high point came for her when she visited a summer camp for young Pioneers, and was lured into joining in a fast polka.

"It was *too* fast," she told me later. "I couldn't keep up with the children." But at least they had had the good fortune to pick on the graceful member of the Nixon family, and the one who knows something about dancing!

We ended our Siberian journey with a stop at the Beloyarsk atomic power station. Here, on the shores of an artificial lake, construction is well under way on an installation which is slated to reach its capacity of 200,000 kilowatts of electricity by 1961.

Admiral Rickover told Mr. Nicolai Kuybyshev, the director, that American scientists would far rather work on peaceful tests of atomic energy than on military projects.

"Your words give me assurance that we may arrive at the stage of doing everything in cooperation," the director replied.

On behalf of President Eisenhower I invited Mr. Kuybyshev and his staff to visit the United States to see our own nuclear installations and our own peaceful applications of atomic power. I hope he can, indeed, come and see for himself.

Back in Moscow I ended my eleven-day visit with an hour-long talk to the Soviet people over the state television network and a radio hookup.[35] *The New York Times* called it "one of the bluntest speeches ever heard by Soviet listeners from a Western visitor."

Actually, I intended not so much to make it blunt as simply to make it as straightforward as I knew how. I felt I should waste no time on diplomatic niceties but get right down to specific cases.

I took it to be my major task to make some contribution, at least, to opening a frank exchange—an exchange of information and ideas—between our two peoples. I did not hope to change overnight the appalling situation of misinformation and lack of understanding—certainly no one speech can do that—or, indeed, to suggest for one moment that there are not deep and significant differences between America and the Soviet Union. Problems—the clash of basic principles—are never solved by glossing them over, by pretending that they do not exist.

We should be under no illusion that mutual understanding—expressions of friendship and good will, the avowed desire of the leaders of world communism for peace, even the exchange of visits between the President and Premier Khrushchev—will suddenly resolve all the differences that divide the Communists and the free world.

But at the same time we must remember this: while understanding alone will not produce peace, misunderstanding can provoke war, war by miscalculation, or by drifting into such rigid positions that the use of force might become inevitable. To avoid this situation we must keep open every possible channel of communication, we must enter into serious and patient negotiations, but always negotiations which are firm on basic principles.

So I used the occasion of my hour on Soviet radio and TV to establish just such communication—to tell the Soviet people,

[35] For full text of this address, see below pp. 235–246.

probably for the first time, that each of them works one day out of four for armaments because of world tensions brought on by fifteen years of Soviet aggression and subversion.

I told them that of course the United States is armed and maintains bases abroad, but not for purposes of aggression against the Soviet Union or any other nation. We mean only to defend ourselves and our allies. We started to build our defenses, indeed, only after the Soviet Union had clearly embarked on a worldwide campaign of subversion and aggression; the Berlin blockade and the war in Korea are the two most dramatic examples.

And I told them this, too: that we do not object if Premier Khrushchev expresses his belief that our grandchildren will live under communism—we object only if he attempts to bring this result about by interfering in our internal affairs.

As for us, we do not say that his grandchildren will or ought to live under a system of free enterprise. The very essence of our belief is that every nation should have the right to choose for itself, free of all coercion, free of outside force, and with full awareness of all the alternatives, the political, economic, and social system under which it wishes to live. We want for other peoples only what we want for ourselves—the freedom to achieve, in their own way, a life of material abundance and, even more basic, of cultural and spiritual richness.

Finally, I told them that the American people wanted a better living standard for the people of the Soviet Union; that if Premier Khrushchev would concentrate his efforts on building a better life for the Soviet people within the Soviet Union, this was an objective we would welcome and support.

But if on the other hand he diverted Soviet energies and resources toward communizing the world, this we would have to resist.

I emphasized that the inevitable result of such a policy would be increased tensions and ultimate misery for the Russians and other peoples as well in the years ahead.

I rejected the negative concept of coexistence, Soviet-style, which means two worlds with two hostile camps, each struggling to impose its system on the other. I submitted in its place the concept of one world where different peoples live under the different systems they choose, but where there is freedom of communication and exchange, and cooperation in achieving mutual goals.

My wife and I have had many exciting experiences during our travels, not only in the Soviet Union but in the fifty-three countries where, since 1953, we have represented President Eisenhower and the American people. There has been much drama on these travels, many gratifying incidents. But there has never been anything to match the experience of our reception in Warsaw.

We arrived on a Sunday afternoon, the exact time unannounced, our route unspecified, with no organized reception of any sort planned by the Polish government. Yet the 10 miles from the airport to the center of Warsaw was lined—literally lined—with a quarter of a million people.

People along every inch of the road, people crowding the city streets, people standing on tiptoe to peer over the heads of those in front of them. People leaning out of apartment windows, waving from trolleys and buses, pressing close to the car when our motorcade slowed to a crawl.

There were the faces, pressed close together, smiling. Every one of them smiling, hands waving, hands clasped above the head and shaken vigorously. Shouts in a language I didn't understand, but carrying a meaning that would have been clear to anyone.

They cheered and shouted their tributes to America, to Eisenhower—even to Nixon. They literally flooded us with flowers. And I could see tears in many eyes—tears, I think, of gratitude that they were thus able to show their devotion to the principles of freedom and independence. I think they were displaying, too, their deep friendship for America as a symbol of freedom and independence in the richest sense of our long tradition and our present dedication.

This was no personal tribute. It was much more than that, and much more important. It was the demonstration by a whole people that, even though they shared a common border with the menacing dictatorship of the U.S.S.R. and although Soviet troops were stationed in their country, they dared to show their feelings, their dedication to the immortal principles of freedom.

Next day one of our party told me that he had had a conversation with a Polish acquaintance shortly after our arrival. He had remarked that Premier Khrushchev, too, on his recent Warsaw visit, had doubtless been greeted with a flood of flowers. "Sure," his Polish friend replied. "But for the American we bought our own flowers."

This story, and our whole Polish experience, simply points up the fact that no amount of censorship or distorted propaganda can weaken the traditional bonds of friendship and affection that join the Polish and the American people together. This is a bond that goes all the way back, of course, to the time of our own Revolution. Clearly, the Polish people have not forgotten it.

And every mile of the way along our route that memorable Sunday in Warsaw served to remind me that we must not forget it either—as we work with all our energy and dedication at the task of securing a world in which men can be free, nations independent, and peoples can live together in peace, harmony, and friendship.

2.   The "Kitchen Debate" [36]

At the gate of the Exhibition, Mr. Khrushchev voiced a gibe about the United States ban on the shipment of strategic goods to the Soviet Union.

Khrushchev: "Americans have lost their ability to trade. Now you have grown older and you don't trade the way you used to. You need to be invigorated."

Nixon: "You need to have goods to trade."

The statesmen went on to look at television and video tape equipment for playing back recordings. Mr. Nixon took a cue from it.

Nixon: "There must be a free exchange of ideas."

Mr. Khrushchev responded with a remark touching on the reporting of his speeches on his recent Polish tour.

Mr. Nixon said he was certain that Mr. Khrushchev's speeches and those of Frol R. Kozlov, First Deputy Premier, had been fully reported in the West.

Khrushchev (indicating cameras recording the scene on video tape): "Then what about this tape?" (Smiling.) "If it is shown in the United States it will be shown in English and I would like a guarantee that there will be a full translation of my remarks."

Mr. Nixon said there would be an English translation of Mr. Khrushchev's remarks and added his hope that all his own remarks in the Soviet Union would be given with full translations in that country.

---

[36] The material in this section is derived from an account of the informal exchanges in Moscow on July 24, 1959, between Vice President Richard Nixon and Premier Nikita S. Khrushchev, compiled from dispatches of *The New York Times,* the Associated Press, United Press International, and Reuters.

Khrushchev: "We want to live in peace and friendship with Americans because we are the two most powerful countries, and if we live in friendship, then other countries will also live in friendship. But if there is a country that is too war-minded we could pull its ears a little and say, 'Don't you dare; fighting is not allowed now.' This is a period of atomic armament; some foolish one could start a war and then even a wise one couldn't finish the war. Therefore, we are governed by this idea in our policy, internal and foreign. How long has America existed? Three hundred years?"

Nixon: "More than one hundred and fifty years."

Khrushchev: "More than one hundred and fifty years? Well, then, we will say America has been in existence for 150 years and this is the level she has reached. We have existed not quite forty-two years and in another seven years we will be on the same level as America.

"When we catch you up, in passing you by, we will wave to you. Then if you wish we can stop and say: Please follow up. Plainly speaking, if you want capitalism you can live that way. That is your own affair and doesn't concern us. We can still feel sorry for you, but since you don't understand us, live as you do understand.

"We are all glad to be here at the Exhibition with Vice President Nixon. I personally, and on behalf of my colleagues, express my thanks for the President's message. I have not as yet read it but I know beforehand that it contains good wishes. I think you will be satisfied with your visit and if—I cannot go on without saying it—if you would not take such a position [37] which has not been thought out thoroughly, as was approved by Congress, your trip would be excellent. But you have churned the water yourselves—why this was necessary God only knows.

[37] Proclamation by the United States government of Captive Nations Week, a week of prayer for peoples enslaved by the Soviet Union.

"What happened? What black cat crossed your path and confused you? But that is your affair; we do not interfere with your problems." (Wrapping his arms about a Soviet workman.) "Does this man look like a slave laborer?" (Waving at others.) "With men with such spirit how can we lose?"

Nixon (pointing to American workmen): "With men like that we are strong. But these men, Soviet and American, work together well for peace, even as they have worked together in building this Exhibition. This is the way it should be.

"Your remarks are in the tradition of what we have come to expect—sweeping and extemporaneous. Later on we will both have an opportunity to speak, and consequently I will not comment on the various points that you raised, except to say this—this color television is one of the most advanced developments in communication that we have.

"I can say that if this competition in which you plan to outstrip us is to do the best for both of our peoples and for peoples everywhere, there must be a free exchange of ideas. After all, you don't know everything. . . ."

Khrushchev: "If I don't know everything, you don't know anything about communism except fear of it."

Nixon: "There are some instances where you may be ahead of us; for example, in the development of the thrust of your rockets for the investigation of outer space; there may be some instances in which we are ahead of you—in color television, for instance."

Khrushchev: "No, we are up with you on this too. We have bested you in one technique and also in the other."

Nixon: "You see, you never concede anything."

Khrushchev: "I do not give up."

Nixon: "Wait till you see the picture. Let's have far more communication and exchange in this very area that we speak of. We should hear you more on our television. You should hear us more on yours."

Khrushchev: "That's a good idea. Let's do it like this. You appear before our people. We will appear before your people. People will see and appreciate this."

Nixon: "There is not a day in the United States when we cannot read what you say. When Kozlov was speaking in California about peace, you were talking here in somewhat different terms. This was reported extensively in the American press. Never make a statement here if you don't want it to be read in the United States. I can promise you every word you say will be translated into English."

Khrushchev: "I doubt it. I want you to give your word that this speech of mine will be heard by the American people."

Nixon (shaking hands on it): "By the same token, everything I say will be translated and heard all over the Soviet Union?"

Khrushchev: "That's agreed."

Nixon: "You must not be afraid of ideas."

Khrushchev: "We are telling you not to be afraid of ideas. We have no reason to be afraid. We have already broken free from such a situation."

Nixon: "Well, then, let's have more exchange of them. We are all agreed on that. All right? All right?"

Khrushchev: "Fine." (Aside.) "Agreed to what? All right, I am in agreement. But I want to stress what I am in agreement with. I know that I am dealing with a very good lawyer. I also want to uphold my own miner's flag so that the coal miners can say, 'Our man does not concede.'"

Nixon: "No question about that."

Khrushchev: "You are a lawyer for capitalism and I am a lawyer for communism. Let's compete."

Nixon: "The way you dominate the conversation you would make a good lawyer yourself. If you were in the United States Senate you would be accused of filibustering."

Khrushchev: "If your reporters will check on the time, they will see who has talked more."

Nixon: "You do all the talking and do not let anyone else talk."

Debate broke out again when the two men reached the model home in the American Exhibition.

Khrushchev (referring to American model home): "You think the Russian people will be dumbfounded to see this? But I tell you all our modern homes have equipment of this sort, and to get a flat you have only to be a Soviet visitor, not a citizen."

Nixon: "We do not claim to astonish the Russian people. We hope to show our diversity and our right to choose. We do not wish to have decisions made at the top by government officials who say that all homes should be built in the same way. Would it not be better to compete in the relative merits of washing machines than in the strength of rockets? Is this the kind of competition you want?"

Khrushchev: "Yes, that's the kind of competition we want, but your generals say we must compete in rockets. Your generals say they are so powerful they can destroy us. We can also show you something so that you will know the Russian spirit. We are strong; we can beat you. But in this respect we can also show you something."

Nixon: "To me you are strong and we are strong. In some ways, you are stronger than we are. In others, we are stronger, but to me it seems that in this day and age to argue who is the stronger completely misses the point. We are both strong, not only from the standpoint of weapons but also from the standpoint of will and spirit.

"No one should ever use his strength to put another in the position where he in effect has an ultimatum. For us to argue who is the stronger misses the point. If war comes we both lose."

Khrushchev: "For the fourth time I have to say I cannot recognize my friend Mr. Nixon. If all Americans agree with you, then who don't we agree [with]? This is what we want."

Nixon: "Anyone who believes the American government does not reflect the people is not an accurate observer of the American scene. I hope the Prime Minister understands all the implications of what I have just said. When you place either one of the powerful nations or any other nations in a position so that they have no choice but to accept dictation or fight, then you are playing with the most destructive thing in the world.

"This is very important in the present world context. It is very dangerous. When we sit down at a conference table it cannot all be one way. One side cannot put an ultimatum to another. It is impossible. But I shall talk to you about this later."

Khrushchev: "Who is raising an ultimatum?"

Nixon: "We will discuss that later."

Khrushchev: "If you have raised the question, why not go on with it now while the people are listening? We know something about politics, too. Let your correspondents compare watches and see who is filibustering. You put great emphasis on *diktat* [dictation]. Our country has never been guided by *diktat*. *Diktat* is a foolish policy."

Nixon: "I am talking about it in the international sense."

Khrushchev: "It sounds to me like a threat. We, too, are giants. You want to threaten—we will answer threats with threats."

Nixon: "That's not my point. We will never engage in threats."

Khrushchev: "You wanted indirectly to threaten me. But we have the means to threaten too."

Nixon: "Who wants to threaten?"

Khrushchev: "You are talking about implications. I have not been. We have the means at our disposal. Ours are better than yours. It is you who want to compete. *Da, da, da.*"

Nixon: "We are well aware that you have the means. To me who is best is not material."

Khrushchev: "You raised the point. We want peace and friendship with all nations, especially with America."

Nixon: "We want peace, too, and I believe that you do also."

Khrushchev: "Yes, I believe that."

Nixon: "I see that you want to build a good life. But I don't think that the cause of peace is helped by reminders that you have greater strength than we do, because this is a threat, too."

Khrushchev: "I was answering your words. You challenged me. Let's argue fairly."

Nixon: "My point was that in today's world it is immaterial which of the two great countries at any particular moment has the advantage. In war, these advantages are illusory. Can we agree on that?"

Khrushchev: "Not quite. Let's not beat around the bush."

Nixon: "I like the way he talks."

Khrushchev: "We want to liquidate all bases from foreign lands. Until that happens we will speak different languages. One who is for putting an end to bases on foreign lands is for peace. One who is against it is for war. We have liquidated our bases, reduced our forces, and offered to make a peace treaty and eliminate the point of friction in Berlin. Until we settle that question, we will talk different languages."

Nixon: "Do you think it can be settled at Geneva?"

Khrushchev: "If we considered it otherwise, we would not have incurred the expense of sending our Foreign Minister to Geneva. Gromyko is not an idler. He is a very good man."

Nixon: "We have great respect for Mr. Gromyko. Some people say he looks like me. I think he is better-looking. I hope it [the Geneva Conference] will be successful."

Khrushchev: "It does not depend on us."

Nixon: "It takes two to make an agreement. You cannot have it all your own way."

Khrushchev: "These are questions that have the same aim. To put an end to the vestiges of war, to make a peace treaty with Germany—that is what we want. It is very bad that we quarrel over the question of war and peace."

Nixon: "There is no question but that your people and you want the government of the United States to be for peace—anyone who thinks that our government is not for peace is not an accurate observer of America. In order to have peace, Mr. Prime Minister, even in an argument between friends, there must be sitting-down around a table. There must be discussion. Each side must find areas where it looks at the other's point of view. The world looks to you today with regard to Geneva. I believe it would be a grave mistake and a blow to peace if it were allowed to fail."

Khrushchev: "This is our understanding as well."

Nixon: "So this is something. The present position is stalemate. Ways must be found to discuss it."

Khrushchev: "The two sides must seek ways of agreement."

In the evening, after formal speeches, Mr. Khrushchev and Mr. Nixon, in departing, stopped by a table laden with glasses of wine. Mr. Khrushchev proposed a toast to "elimination of all military bases in foreign lands." Mr. Nixon sidestepped, suggested they drink to peace instead.

Khrushchev: "If you're not one to eliminate bases, then I'll make a toast."

Nixon: "He doesn't like American wine."

Khrushchev: "I like American wine—not its policy."

Nixon (aside): "I've always heard he's a vigorous defender of his policy, not only officially but unofficially."

Khrushchev: "I will defend the real policy, which is to assure peace. How can peace be assured when we are surrounded by military bases?"

Nixon: "We will talk about that later. We will drink to talking. When we are talking we are not fighting."

Khrushchev: "We drink to talking."

Mr. Khrushchev suggested they drink to several women standing by.

Nixon: "A good nonpolitical drink."

Bystander: "A hundred years of life for Mr. Khrushchev."

Nixon: "I will drink to that. We disagree with your policy, but we want you to be of good health. May you live to be a hundred years old."

Mr. Khrushchev said he would accept the toast, adding: "At ninety-nine years of age we shall discuss the question further. Why should we be in haste?"

Nixon: "Ninety-nine years [and] you will still be in power?— and without an election?"

3. *America Accepts the Challenge* [38]

I am honored on behalf of President Eisenhower to open this American Exhibition in Moscow.

Mrs. Nixon and I were among the many thousands of Americans who were privileged to visit the splendid Soviet Exhibition in New York, and we want to take this opportunity to congratulate the people of the U.S.S.R. for the great achievements and progress so magnificently portrayed by your Exhibition.

We, in turn, hope that many thousands of Soviet citizens will take advantage of this opportunity to learn about life in the United States by visiting our Exhibition.

Of course we both realize that no exhibition can portray a complete picture of all aspects of life in great nations like the U.S.S.R. and the United States.

[38] This section consists of the Vice President's remarks on the occasion of the opening of the American National Exhibition in Moscow, Sokolniki Park. July 24, 1959.

Among the questions which some might raise with regard to our Exhibition are these: To what extent does this Exhibition accurately present life in the United States as it really is? Can only the wealthy people afford the things exhibited here? What about the inequality, the injustice, the other weaknesses which are supposed to be inevitable in a capitalist society?

As Mr. Khrushchev often says: "You can't leave a word out of a song." Consequently, in the limited time I have, I would like to try to answer some of these questions so that you may get an accurate picture of what America is really like.

Let us start with some of the things in this Exhibit. You will see a house, a car, a television set—each the newest and most modern of its type we produce. But can only the rich in the United States afford such things? If this were the case we would have to include in our definition of rich the millions of America's wage earners.

Let us take, for example, our 16 million factory workers. The average weekly wage of a factory worker in America is $90.54. With this income he can buy and afford to own a house, a television set, and a car in the price range of those you will see in this Exhibit. What is more, the great majority of American wage earners have done exactly that.

Putting it another way, there are 44 million families in the United States. Twenty-five million of these families live in houses or apartments that have as much or more floor space than the one you see in this Exhibit. Thirty-one million families own their own homes and the land on which they are built. America's 44 million families own a total of 56 million cars, 50 million television sets, and 143 million radio sets. And they buy an average of 9 dresses and suits and 14 pairs of shoes per family per year.

Why do I cite these figures? Not because they indicate that the American people have more automobiles, TV sets, or houses than the people of the U.S.S.R.

In fairness we must recognize that our country industrialized sooner than the Soviet Union. And Americans are happy to note that Mr. Khrushchev has set a goal for the Soviet economy of catching up in the production of consumer goods.

We welcome this kind of competition because when we engage in it, no one loses—everyone wins, as the living standards of people throughout the world are raised to higher levels. It also should be pointed out that while we may be ahead of you as far as these items are concerned, you are ahead of us in other fields—for example, in the size of the rockets you have developed for the exploration of outer space.

But what these statistics do dramatically demonstrate is this: that the United States, the world's largest capitalist country, has from the standpoint of distribution of wealth come closest to the ideal of prosperity for all in a classless society.

As our revered Abraham Lincoln said, "... We do not propose any war upon capital; we do wish to allow the humblest man an equal chance to get rich with everybody else."

The 67 million American wage earners are not the downtrodden masses depicted by the critics of capitalism in the latter part of the nineteenth and early part of the twentieth century. They hold their heads high as they proudly enjoy the highest standard of living of any people in the world's history.

The caricature of capitalism as a predatory, monopolist-dominated society, is as hopelessly out of date, as far as the United States is concerned, as a wooden plow.

This does not mean that we have solved all of our problems. Many of you have heard about the problem of unemployment in the United States. What is not so well known is that the average period that these unemployed were out of work even during our recent recession was less than three months. And during that period the unemployed had an average income from unemployment insurance funds of $131.49 per month. The day has passed in the United States when the unemployed were left to shift for themselves.

The same can be said for the aged, the sick, the others who

are unable to earn enough to provide an adequate standard of living. An expanded program of social security combined with other government and private programs provides aid and assistance for those who are unable to care for themselves. For example, the average retired couple on social security in the United States receives an income of $116 per month apart from the additional amounts they receive from private pensions and savings accounts.

What about the strikes which take place in our economy, the latest example of which is the steel strike that is going on? The answer is that here we have a firsthand example of how a free economy works. The worker's right to join with other workers in a union and to bargain collectively with management is recognized and protected by law. No man or woman in the United States can be forced to work for wages he considers to be inadequate or under conditions he believes are unsatisfactory.

Another problem which causes us concern is that of racial discrimination in our country. We are making great progress in solving this problem but we shall never be satisfied until we make the American ideal of equality of opportunity a reality for every citizen, regardless of his race, creed, or color.

We have other problems in our society, but we are confident that for us our system of government provides the best means for solving them. But the primary reason we believe this is not because we have an economy which builds more than 1 million houses, produces 6 million cars and 6 million television sets per year.

Material progress is important but the very heart of the American ideal is that "Man does not live by bread alone." To us, progress without freedom, to use a common expression, is like "potatoes without fat."

Let me give you some examples of what freedom means to us.

President Eisenhower is one of the most popular men ever to hold that high office in our country. Yet never an hour or a day goes by in which criticism of him and his policies cannot be read in our newspapers, heard on our radio and television, or in the halls of Congress.

And he would not have it any other way. The fact that our people can and do say anything they want about a government official, and the fact that in our elections, as this voting machine in our Exhibit illustrates, every voter has a free choice between those who hold public office and those who oppose them, make ours a true people's government.

We trust the people. We constantly submit big decisions to the people. Our history convinces us that over the years the people have been right much more often than they have been wrong.

As an indication of the extent of this freedom and of our faith in our own system, forty hours of radio broadcasts from the Soviet Union can be heard without jamming in the United States each day, and over a million and a half copies of Soviet publications are purchased in our country each year.

Let us turn now to freedom of religion. Under our Constitution no church or religion can be supported by the state. An American can either worship in the church of his choice or choose to go to no church at all if he wishes. Acting with this complete freedom of choice, 103 million of our citizens are members of 308,000 American churches.

We also cherish the freedom to travel, both within our country and outside the United States. Within our country we live and travel where we please without travel permits, internal passports, or police registration. We also travel freely abroad. For example, 11 million Americans will travel to other countries during this year, including 10,000 to the Soviet Union. We look forward to the day when millions of Soviet citizens will travel to our own and other countries in this way.

Time will not permit me to tell you of all of the features of American life, but in summary I think these conclusions can objectively be stated.

The great majority of Americans like our system of government. Much as we like it, however, we would not impose it on anyone else. We believe that people everywhere should have a right to choose the form of government they want.

There is another characteristic of the American people which I know impresses itself on any visitor to our country. As Mr. Mikoyan and Mr. Kozlov both pointed out after their visits to the United States, the American people are a peace-loving people. There are a number of reasons for this attitude. As this Exhibition so eloquently demonstrates, we Americans enjoy an extraordinarily high standard of living.

There is nothing we want from any other people except the right to live in peace and friendship with them.

After fighting two world wars we did not ask for or receive an acre of land from any other people. We have no desire to impose our rule on other lands today.

Our hearts go out to Mr. Khrushchev, who lost a son; to Mr. Kozlov, who lost two brothers; and to the millions of other Soviet mothers and fathers, brothers and sisters, sons and daughters who mourn for their loved ones who died defending their homeland.

But while it is generally recognized that the American people want peace, I realize that it has sometimes been charged that our government does not share the attitude of our people. Nothing could be further from the truth.

For seven years I have sat in the high councils of our government and I can tell you that the primary aim of our discussions has been to find ways that we could use our strength in behalf of peace throughout the world.

Let me tell you of the background of some of those who participate in our policy discussions. The Secretary of State lost his brother in World War I. I saw boys as close to me as brothers die on barren islands 4,000 miles from home in World War II. No man in the world today has more knowledge of war and is more dedicated to peace than President Eisenhower.

Those who claim that the policies of the American government do not represent and are not supported by the American people are engaging in a completely inaccurate and dangerous form of self-deception. Any Administration which follows policies which do not reflect the views of our people on major issues runs the risk of defeat at the next election. When our elected officials cease to represent the people, the people have the power to replace them with others who do. The reason the leaders of both our major political parties are united in supporting President Eisenhower's foreign policy is that they are reflecting the views of a people who are united behind these policies.

The government and people of the United States are as one in their devotion to the cause of peace.

But dedication to peace, good will, and human brotherhood should never be mistaken for weakness, softness, and fear.

Much as we want peace, we will fight to defend our country and our way of life just as you have fought so courageously to defend your homeland throughout your history.

The peace we want and the peace the world needs is not the peace of surrender but the peace of justice; not peace by ultimatum but peace by negotiation.

The leaders of our two great nations have tremendous responsibilities if peace is to be maintained in our time.

We cannot and should not gloss over the fact that we have some great and basic differences between us. What we must constantly strive to do is to see that those differences are discussed and settled at the conference table and not on the battlefield.

And until such settlements are agreed to, our leaders must exercise the greatest restraint, patience, and understanding in their actions and their statements. They must do nothing which might provoke a war no one wants.

The fact that one of us may have a bigger bomb, a faster plane, or a more powerful rocket than the other at any particular time no longer adds up to an advantage. For we have reached the point in world history where the biblical injunction "They that take the sword shall perish with the sword" is literally true today.

The nation which starts a war today will destroy itself. Completely apart from any retaliatory action which might be taken by a nation which is attacked, the deadly dust from radioactive bombs used in an attack will be carried by the winds back to the homeland of the aggressor.

With both of our great nations holding this terrible power in our hands neither must ever put the other in a position where he has no choice but to fight or surrender. No nation in the world today is strong enough to issue an ultimatum to another without running the risk of self-destruction.

The Soviet Exhibition in New York and the American Exhibition which we open tonight are dramatic examples of what a great future lies in store for all of us if we can devote the tremendous energies of our peoples and the resources of our countries to the ways of peace rather than the ways of war.

The last half of the twentieth century can be the darkest or the brightest page in the history of civilization. The decision is in our hands to make. The genius of the men who produced the magnificent achievements represented by these two Exhibitions can be directed either to the destruction of civilization or to the creation of the best life that men have ever enjoyed on this earth.

As I have said on previous occasions, let us expand the idea of peaceful competition which Mr. Khrushchev has often enunciated. Let us extend this competition to include the spiritual as well as the material aspects of our civilization. Let us compete not in how to take lives but in how to save them. Let us work for victory not in war but for the victory of plenty over poverty, of health over disease, of understanding over ignorance, wherever they exist in the world.

Above all, let us find more and more areas where we can substitute cooperation for competition in achieving our goal of a fuller, freer, richer life for every man, woman, and child on this earth.

4. *A Talk to the Russian People* [39]

I first want to express my appreciation to the government of the U.S.S.R. for giving me an opportunity to speak to the people of this country by radio and television just as Mr. Kozlov and Mr. Mikoyan spoke to the American people on their visits to my country.

I realize that nine days is much too brief a time for a visitor to spend in this great country. But in that period I have had the opportunity of having extended and frank discussions with Mr. Khrushchev and other leaders of your government. I have visited Leningrad, Siberia and the Urals and I have had the privilege of meeting thousands of people in all walks of life.

What I would like to do tonight is to answer for the millions of people who are listening to this program some of the questions which were asked me over and over again on this trip so that you may get a true picture of the policies of the American government and people.

I should like to begin by answering a question which I often

---

[39] This section consists of the Vice President's remarks to the Soviet nation delivered in an unprecedented radio-television address from Moscow. August 1, 1959. (This address was reprinted in Soviet newspapers.)

heard: What are my impressions of this country, and its people?

While my visit was brief I did have a chance in addition to visiting this great capital city of Moscow to see the beauty and culture of Leningrad whose brave people won the admiration of the world for their heroic defense of their city during the war; to savor the inspiring pioneer spirit of Novosibirsk; to witness firsthand the thriving productivity of the factory complex of the Urals. I was greatly impressed by the efficient modern equipment of your factories; your magnificent ballets in Leningrad and Novosibirsk; by the competitive drive for progress which is evident on every side.

But most of all I was impressed by your people; after all, the greatest asset of a country is not its forests, its factories or its farms but its people.

These are some of the characteristics of the Soviet people which I particularly noted on this trip.

First, their capacity for hard work, their vitality; their intense desire to improve their lot, to get ahead, is evident everywhere.

There was another feature about the Soviet people which I noted that may surprise you and that is in how many respects you are like us Americans. We are similar in our love of humor —we laugh at the same jokes. The people of your frontier East have much the same spirit of what was our frontier West. We have a common love of sports; the name of Vasily Kuznetsov, your great decathlon champion, is known in the United States as well as it is in the Soviet Union. We are both a hospitable, friendly people. When we meet each other we tend to like each other personally, as so many of our soldiers who met during the last great war can attest.

Above all, the American people and the Soviet people are as one in their desire for peace. And our desire for peace is not because either of us is weak. On the contrary, each of us is strong and respects the strength the other possesses.

This means that if we are to have peace it must be a just peace based on mutual respect rather than the peace of surrender or dictation by either side. Putting it bluntly, both of our peoples want peace but both of us also possess great strength and much as we want peace neither of us can or will tolerate being pushed around.

That is why I was so surprised at a question that was asked me by a worker on the new scientific center outside of Novosibirsk. My heart went out to him as he told me that he had been wounded in World War II and that his father and mother had been killed by bombs. But then he said, "I don't believe you when you say America is for peace."

Nothing he could have said could have astonished or saddened me more.

And so to the millions of Soviet people who suffered or lost their loved ones in war, and to all of those in this great country who want peace, I say tonight, if you doubt that the American government and the American people are as dedicated to peace as you are, look at our record, examine our policies and you can reach only one conclusion—only aggressor nations have anything to fear from the United States of America.

We have fought in two World Wars and have demanded and received not an acre of territory or a cent in reparation. We enjoy the highest standard of living of any people in the world's history, and there is nothing whatever that we want from any other people in the world except to live in peace and friendship with them. No leader in the world today could be more dedicated to peace than our President. As his brother, who has honored us by making this visit with us, can tell you, President Eisenhower's whole life is proof of the stark but simple truth—that no one hates war more than one who has seen a lot of it.

We know as do you that in this age of nuclear weapons it is impossible for either of our nations to launch an attack which would not bring terrible destruction to itself.

In this age any leader who is so insane even to think of starting a war should well heed your proverb—"Do not dig a pit for another; you may fall into it yourself."

Why then is there any doubt that the American government and people are just as dedicated to peace as the people of the U.S.S.R.? I think part of the answer is to be found in another question which was often asked of me on this trip and which Mr. Khrushchev, himself, raised in this manner in his speech on July 28 at Dnepropetrovsk. "If you believe in the peaceful intentions of our country, why do you continue the arms race, why do you construct new military bases around our borders?"

In answering this question, let me first point out that these bases are not maintained for purposes of attacking you but for purposes of defending ourselves and our allies.

Why did we think it was necessary to set up bases? Let us look at the record. We disarmed rapidly after World War II. Then came a series of events which threatened our friends abroad as well as ourselves. The Berlin blockade and the war in Korea are typical of the actions which led the United States and our allies to rearm so that we could defend ourselves against aggression.

We must also remember that these events occurred before the 20th Party Congress changed the line to the one Mr. Khrushchev enunciated again in his speech at Dnepropetrovsk—that communism will now try to achieve its international objectives by peaceful means rather than by force. I could cite statement after statement made by previous leaders of the U.S.S.R. which advocated and threatened the use of force against non-Communist countries in order to achieve Communist objectives.

A striking illustration of why we maintain bases and strong military forces is the fact that one-fourth of the entire production of the U.S.S.R. goes into armaments. This, in effect, means that every worker in the Soviet Union works one day out of four for armaments. And we in our country are also bearing a heavy burden of armaments. Think what it could mean to both of our countries if we could lift this burden from the backs of our people.

Some may ask, why don't we get rid of the bases since the Soviet government declares today that it has only peaceful intentions? The answer is that whenever the fear and suspicion that caused us and our allies to take measures for collective self-defense are removed, the reason for our maintaining bases will be removed. In other words, the only possible solution of this problem lies in mutual rather than unilateral action leading toward disarmament.

Another question which was often asked was—why won't the United States agree to stop the tests of atomic weapons? The answer in a nutshell is that the question is not whether we both should enter into an agreement to stop tests but whether that agreement is one which will make sure that the tests actually are stopped.

That is why we say that if both sides honestly want to stop tests, we must first agree to set up inspection procedures in both of our countries which will make certain that the agreement is not violated. We believe this position is the only one that gives assurance of accomplishing the objective of stopping tests rather than just signing an agreement to do so.

We are encouraged by the fact that at least in this area we are presently engaged in serious negotiations which have made some progress. I know that I express the sentiments of the people of both of our countries when I say that I am hopeful that these negotiations will finally end in agreement.

Another question that has often been asked me went something like this: "The United States says it is for peace, but what the world wants are deeds not words, and the United States is short on deeds and long on words."

Nothing could be further from the truth. It is possible that many of you listening to me are not aware of the positive programs the United States has proposed which were designed to contribute to peace. Let me tell you about just a few of them and what happened to them:

We had a monopoly on the atomic bomb when on June 14, 1946, we submitted the Baruch plan for international control of atomic energy. What happened? It was rejected by the U.S.S.R.

Under Article 43 of the United Nations Charter, provision was made for the establishment of the United Nations Armed Forces to keep the peace. On June 4, 1947, we made the first of many requests that agreement be reached. What happened? All have been rejected by the U.S.S.R.

At the Summit Conference in Geneva on July 21, 1955, President Eisenhower made his offer of open skies aerial inspection. What happened? It was rejected by the U.S.S.R.

On May 1, 1958, the United States offered an Arctic aerial inspection plan to protect both nations from surprise attack. What happened? It was rejected by the U.S.S.R.

I realize that your government has indicated reasons for its rejection of each of these proposals. I do not list these proposals for the purpose of warming over past history but simply to demonstrate the initiative that our government has taken to reduce tensions and to find peaceful solutions for differences between us.

I realize that my answers to these questions indicate that there are some very basic differences between us. But let me emphasize at the same time that the very fact that we have not made as much progress as we would like in the past in settling our differences is the strongest reason for us to redouble our efforts to create better understanding between our two countries; to remove fear, suspicion and misconceptions where they exist, and thereby, to pave the way for discussions and eventual settlement by agreement of some of the basic conflicts between us.

We should both frankly recognize that we have some very real differences that are not easily settled. But two men who are friends can settle an argument between them without using their fists and two nations who want to be friends can do so without war.

I should like to suggest tonight some practical steps which will contribute to the cause of peace to which we are both dedicated.

First there are some positive things we can do which will create better understanding between us.

We can start by removing the language barrier. Here is one place where you are ahead of us. I was amazed at the number of people I met on this trip who were studying English. What we need are millions of American students who understand Russian and millions of Soviet students who understand English.

Both the exchange of persons and the cultural exchange programs should not only be continued but sharply expanded. The more Americans who visit and get to know first-hand the people of the Soviet Union and the more Soviet citizens who do the same in the United States, the better understanding we shall have.

I believe also that visits by officials like the ones Mr. Mikoyan and Mr. Kozlov made to the United States and which I have just concluded can provide the means of frank and full discussion of some of our problems and the development of solutions for them. Consequently, we should explore ways of increasing contacts of this type.

Most important of all, we need a much freer exchange of information between our two countries so that misconceptions we may have about you and that you have about us may be removed. I was rather surprised that Mr. Khrushchev should raise a question about the failure of the Western press to report adequately one of his recent statements. I would estimate that at least 100 of Mr. Khrushchev's words are printed in our American press for every one word of President Eisenhower's speeches printed in the Soviet press.

Perhaps this is an area where the cause of better understanding would be served if we had a more equal exchange. Let us agree that all of Mr. Khrushchev's speeches on foreign policy be printed in the United States and that all of President Eisenhower's speeches on foreign policy be printed in the Soviet Union.

Why not go further and set up regular radio and television broadcasts by Mr. Khrushchev to the American people in return for President Eisenhower having the same privilege to talk to the Soviet people?

Let us put a stop to the jamming of broadcasts so that the Soviet people may hear broadcasts from our country just as the American people can hear forty hours of broadcasts a day from the Soviet Union. And let us have a freer flow of newspapers and magazines so that the Soviet people can buy American newspapers and magazines here just as we Americans purchased over one and one-half million Soviet publications in last year alone.

I recognize that freedom of information can be abused and that neither of us is free from blame in this respect. The press, radio, television, and other means of communication such as film studios, have a heavy responsibility for maintaining the spirit of truth and for preventing misinformation. In the final analysis the misrepresentation of facts or distortion of the truth defeats itself. Let me give you an example from an experience that occurred to me on this trip.

There was a report in *Trud* to the effect that on the morning after I arrived in Moscow I tried to give money to a poor Soviet citizen, with the hope that American press photographers might take pictures of the incident and send them around the world. There was not a shred of truth to this story.

Here is what actually happened. On an early morning visit to the Danilovskiy Market, I had talked to scores of people and received a most friendly welcome. As I was about to leave, several of the people asked me for tickets to the American Exhibition. I told them I did not have any with me, but that I would be glad to buy some tickets for those present who wanted to attend the Exhibition. One of the group explained that it was not a question of their not having money for the tickets, but simply a question of their not being able to obtain them. I told him I would be glad to check into the matter and see if I could get tickets for him.

These are the simple facts as far as this incident was concerned, and I can only add that all irresponsible reporters should never forget that in the end the truth always catches up with a lie.

Through this greater exchange of information between our two peoples we not only learn from each other and improve our way of life but we reduce the suspicion, the mistrust, the fear and misunderstanding and assure the understanding and friendship which will lead to the peace we all want. That is why, to me, the concept of coexistence is completely inadequate and negative. Coexistence implies that the world must be divided into two hostile camps with a wall of hate and fear between.

What we need today is not two worlds but one world where different peoples choose the economic and political systems which they want, but where there is free communication among all the peoples living on this earth.

Let us expand the concept of open skies. What the world also needs are open cities, open minds and open hearts.

Let us have peaceful competition not only in producing the best factories but in producing better lives for our people.

Let us cooperate in our exploration of outer space. As a worker told me in Novosibirsk, let us go to the moon together.

Let our aim be not victory over other peoples but the victory of all mankind over hunger, want, misery and disease, wherever it exists in the world.

I realize that this era of peaceful competition and even cooperation seems like an impossible dream when we consider the present differences we have between us. But the leaders of our countries can help make this dream come true. So far as the leader of our country is concerned, I can assure you that President Eisenhower has no objective to which he is more dedicated.

As far as Mr. Khrushchev is concerned, as I am sure you know, we disagree sharply on political and economic philosophy and on many world problems. But these characteristics are evident to anyone who meets him—He is a self-made man who worked his way up from the bottom; he is an articulate spokesman for the economic system in which he believes; he has immense drive; in sum, he is one of those individuals who, whether you agree with him or disagree with him, is a born leader of men. Because he has these unique qualities and because the decisions he makes will affect not only the 200 million people of the U.S.S.R. but the 3 billion people on this earth, he carries a tremendous responsibility on his shoulders.

I would not be so presumptuous as to try to give him advice on how he should fulfill that responsibility. But could I relate something that I noted on the trip I have just completed? In every factory and on hundreds of billboards I saw this slogan, "Let us work for the victory of communism."

If Mr. Khrushchev means by this slogan working for a better life for the people within the Soviet Union, that is one thing. If, on the other hand, he means the victory of communism over the United States and other countries, this is a horse of a different color. For we have our own ideas as to what system is best for us.

If he devotes his immense energies and talents to building a better life for the people of his own country, Mr. Khrushchev can go down in history as one of the greatest leaders the Soviet people have ever produced. But if he diverts the resources and talents of his people to the objective of promoting the communization of countries outside the Soviet Union, he will only assure that both he and his people will continue to live in an era of fear, suspicion and tension.

The Geneva Conference is a case in point. It would not be proper for me to comment on the specific proposals that are pending before that conference at this time. But agreements between great powers cannot be reached unless they take into account the views and interests of all parties concerned. I was encouraged to note in my conversations with Mr. Khrushchev that he recognizes this fact and agrees that a successful outcome of this conference could be a great step forward in settling some of the problems I have discussed tonight.

I have one final thought to add. Mr. Khrushchev predicted that our grandchildren would live under communism. He reiterated this to me in our talks last Sunday.

Let me say that we do not object to his saying this will happen. We only object if he tries to bring it about.

And this is my answer to him. I do not say that your grandchildren will live under capitalism. We prefer our system. But the very essence of our belief is that we do not and will not try to impose our system on anybody else. We believe that you and all other peoples on this earth should have the right to choose the kind of economic or political system which best fits your particular problems without any foreign intervention.

As I leave your country, I shall never forget an incident that occurred as I was driving through your beautiful Ural Mountains. A group of children on the side of the road threw wild flowers into my car and cried in English the words "friendship," "friendship." Mr. Zhukov told me that the first word children who study English are taught is the word "friendship." There could be no more eloquent expression of the attitude of the Soviet people, an attitude which we share in common with you.

Finally, may I express on behalf of my wife and myself, and all the members of our party, our deep appreciation for the warm friendship and boundless hospitality we have found everywhere we have gone in the Soviet Union. I pledge to you that in the years to come I shall devote my best efforts to the cause of peace with justice for all the peoples of the world.

Mr. Nixon's Life in Brief

January 9, 1913—Born in Yorba Linda, California

1919–1930	Attended public schools in California; worked in family grocery store.
1930–1934	Attended Whittier College; president of student body; graduated second in his class.
1934–1937	Attended Duke University Law School; president of Law School student body; graduated with honors.
1937–1941	Admitted to California Bar; joined Whittier law firm; became a general partner within one year.
1940	Married Patricia Ryan, a Whittier schoolteacher; two daughters; Patricia, born 1946, and Julie, born 1948.
1942	Joined legal staff of the Office of Price Administration, Washington, D.C.
1942–1946	Served in U.S. Navy; South Pacific Combat Air Transport Command; left active duty in 1946 as lieutenant commander.
1946, 1948	Elected to U.S. House of Representatives over five-term opponent by more than 15,000 votes; reelected as candidate on both Republican and Democratic tickets.
	Member, House Labor Committee, House Un-American Activities Committee.
	Supported passage of the Taft-Hartley Law over Presidential veto.
	Instrumental in exposure of Alger Hiss through intensive investigation of Whittaker Chambers' testimony.
	Made on-the-spot study of conditions in Europe and administration of U.S. funds abroad as member of the select Herter Committee.

1950   Elected to U.S. Senate over Helen Gahagan
               Douglas by 700,000 votes—the highest plurality
               of any Senator running that year.

               Member of Senate Labor Committee and Gov-
               ernment Operations Committee.

1952, 1956   Elected and reelected Vice President of the
               United States.

               Domestic Responsibilities:
               President of the Senate.

               Statutory member of National Security Coun-
               cil, and member of the Cabinet. Presided over
               both in the absence of the President.

               Chairman, President's Committee on Govern-
               ment Contracts.

               Chairman, Cabinet Committee on Price Sta-
               bility for Economic Growth.

               Assumed additional responsibility during the
               President's illness on three occasions.

               Role in Foreign Affairs:
               On seven separate occasions was sent to criti-
               cal areas abroad as the President's personal
               ambassador of good will. Since 1953 he has
               visited 55 countries, traveling more than
               150,000 miles. He is personally acquainted
               with most of the world's leaders.

Index